NINE POWERS TO

TRANSFORM YOUR LIFE

Para vos Cloe;
que sigas inspirando
a millones y a
uns por día :)
Sos Maravillosa!

NINE POWERS TO TRANSFORM YOUR LIFE

Espero conocerte
en persona pronto

Con Amor y
Alegría ☼

Nicolás Nóbile

Cover Art & Design: Ramiro Cazaux

ISBN: 978-0-615-21821-2

Printed in U.S.A.

To Wayne W. Dyer

Thank you for inspiring me to explore my talents

and express my inner music to the world.

CONTENTS

Nine Powers
to Transform Your Life

ACKNOWLEDGMENTS

I want to acknowledge my spiritual counterparts, my soul-mates who are the sacred guidance source from which this book was originally inspired. To my teachers who taught me discipline, unconditional love and reminded me always that there's nothing I cannot achieve.

There are many people who reminded me the greatest lesson of all, to love. Arielle Nóbile, a soul mate who encouraged me to return to writing and to develop my power of purpose. Without your support this book could have never been done. My eternal appreciation to your wonderful heart, I love you.

To my friends who remind me, all the time, that there is no distance that can interfere with our desires to enjoy our adventures: Ramiro Cazaux, Evelina Morales, Cristian Nuñez, Juan Manuel Rios, Joris Prikken, Steve Gehring, Gabriel Sanchez, Carlos Omar Schargorodsky (Popey), David Gonzalez, Leonidas Paganini, Jose Garciarena, Lucas Fornasari, Evangelina y Emiliano Murillo, Guillermo Cedres (Toto), Maria Ines Salzman, Bety Soliz, Elisa Terragno, Ivan Gomez, Catherine Cruz, Dalina Vainstein, Gladys Strasser, Clara y Sofia Gutierrez, Soledad Navarro, Fabiola Dus De Zan, Noelia Gauna.

i

I would like to extend my profound gratitude to Romina Boch, who translated this book written half in English and half in Spanish and who inspired me to be an alchemist writer.

Thank you, Kelly Connolly, and Arielle Nóbile for your contributions and patience to my English writing process.

I want to express my deep appreciation to my blood family: to my brother German who helped me develop my power of purpose by inviting me and helping me start my new life in Chicago, USA, to my brother Freddy who inspired me to work from an early age and helped me achieve some of my goals. To my parents Angel and Marta who taught me the importance of being independent.

There are many souls that shared amazing contributions with me, some of them are gone into another realm of life, some of them lost contact for many reasons, but I keep them in my heart and I want to express my gratitude for their beautiful spirits. I know we will meet again at some point: Ignacio Conde, Giselle Ruiz, Julie Rihani, Dario Valli, Milca Neuwirt, Helmut Schuster, Grissel Colmenares, Mariana Lemiña, Emanuel Dezorzi, Marta Ines Olaechea, Natalia Derudi, Victor Acosta, Claudia Bacarat, Silvana Bereciartu, Leticia Doorman, Facundo Balerdi, Marito y Mariano Retamar, Dario y Sabrina Nissero, Carin Dhaouadi, Gabriel Muñoz, Florencia and Anibal Krasser, Hernan Isasi, Carla Melo, Cristian Giraldez, Martin Jurado, Gustavo Garcia (Samurai), Terecita Nazer, Victor Peruzzo, Waldemar Heiler, Julio Vidal, Analia Laborde, Rachel

Reichlin, Eduardo Catan, Dharma Oriach, Lillian Lovas, Victoria y Bibiana Ferrea, Lorenzo Tello, Mariano Olivera, Mario Santoscoy, Iliana Pisarro, Jon Stoper, William Basalo, Ardvind Yadav, Rosanna and Rosaura De La Rosa, Ladislao Masztalerz, Federico Peter, Marivi Vignola, and Freddy Borrajo.

I wish to express my genuine appreciation to some of my wonderful teachers: Adrian Fratantoni, Claudia Piquet, Norma Beatriz Soliz, Accem Scott, Carol Bridges, Alan Uretz, Gustavo Stiepovich, and Cristina Chiriguini.

I would like to express my deep affection and appreciation to the many souls that have blessed me with the powers I am describing in this book, without them this book could not be possible. People who shared their spirits' purposes with me and who encouraged me to trust my inner guidance and follow my heart's desires: Ivan Gomez, Delfina Larrivey, Florencia Garciarena, and Sabrina Spiazzi.

I want to recognize my gratitude to the people in Chicago who have contributed to the realization of this book: Julia Marcos, Arielle Nóbile, Ruthann Gagnon, Ramiro Cazaux, and Kelly Connolly.

Finally I would like to acknowledge my students, whose privacy I respect, who taught me what I needed to learn the most, without their contributions I could not be continuously polishing my skills.

Thank you, God.

Prologue

The purpose of this book is to bring you the transcendental meaning of your inner guidance. It is intended to unravel your full potential to manifest anything you consider missing in your life. The need for transformation depends on the quality of your feelings. If you think you lack something in your life, this book can help you transform your reality.

You will discover in the chapters to come how to use the powers you have to vibrate accordingly with the happiness and harmony you seek.

Do you dare to discover your wonderful potential? To experience the magical world of infinite possibilities?

You have the chance—and that is why you have this book in your hands—to explore the meaning of your adventure here on Earth, and this book will inspire you to unveil your purpose and make your way towards your goals confidently.

Every step you have taken until now has created the path that has led you to this moment of introspection, where you needed to be to discover your divine potential. Everything you are experiencing is exactly what you are manifesting with your co-creation power. Right now, as you read these lines, something special is happening within you. An innate force begins to be attracted to express the integrity of your being, therefore inviting the opportunities that will come to your experience, revealing to you what you need to find out to enjoy your talents. These opportunities are the ones that will provide you the experiences that will keep you active and in harmony with your purpose. If you are determined to keep going forward towards your dreams, even if you can only see the first steps ahead, that will be enough. It is in your confidence in this magnificent Universe of possibilities that you will find the opportunities to let your power of expression take place. Finally, you will see you can achieve your goals, fulfil your purpose, and trust your own guidance to transform your life, today and forever.

You are more powerful than you think. If every time you learn something you realize everything you still have to discover, then the motivation and the enthusiasm of exploration will propel the game. You will be getting deeper into the most transcendental secrets of this Universe of infinite possibilities instead of believing you already know everything you need to. You will find out that there is not and there have never been obstacles, only opportunities.

Make the most of them!

Introduction

Looking back into my life experiences, I could see the attraction power of my emotions and thoughts that led me to perceive an unwanted reality. However, a force within me always knew and alerted me to walk down the path of love. What was this force? Where did it come from? The link between my level of perception and the actual reality always amazed me. Things are never as they seem to be. Why, being full of talents, do we experience so much fear?

An inner voice always called me back to a place where only miracles were possible, reminding me of my capabilities of living my life with purpose. Is this voice the voice of God? Am I able to communicate with the Divine Source we all come from? Are you?

With *Nine Powers to Transform Your Life* my intention is to touch your soul with a message of peace and compassion. To remind you that you can transform your life with Nine Powers you already have and to invite you to encourage others to awaken theirs.

You are a powerful being. You have chosen to walk the

spiritual path and along with you there are other 'angels,' other messengers, walking, just like you, the extra mile.

We live here and now. The past cannot lead you anywhere; it can only serve as experience. Even so, remember that your perceptions of the past can be transmuted with your spirit's wisdom. Perceiving comes from beliefs while wisdom comes from experiencing the knowledge you already possess—from the powers within.

It was during my search for answers and in the discovery I made about perception and reality that this next story I will tell you took place. It led me to become an inspirational writer and teacher.

The Story

Since I was a kid I have been interested in subjects like compassion development, the practice of unconditional mildness, spiritual enrichment, consciousness awakening through knowledge and its practice to reach wisdom.

I could not bear to see animals mistreated, the agony of war, slander that always ended up affecting the related victim, indiscriminate violence, racism, corrupt governments, and everything that could lead us to living hell. Everything that would separate us, instead of uniting us, as children of the same land.

When I left my small hometown to move to Buenos Aires and start medical school I experienced a series of illusions that conditioned this significant social and environmental transition. Breaking up with my first girlfriend, after three years of dating, which was an eternity to me at that stage, only made things worse.

Buenos Aires was very different. It seemed so much bigger and intimidating. People seemed to live at a much-accelerated rate. The traffic was chaotic and the air seemed thicker and poisoned with stress.

My perception was, at that time, manipulated by very

interrelated fears—fear of isolation, of change, fear of not having enough financial resources, fear of a new lifestyle that seemed so stressful, fear of not being accepted, and fear of feeling afraid. I remember my illusions were based on another era, another dimension. It was like I was longing to live in some other period of time that was more in line with my belief system, my feelings and my opinion of what it meant to live on this planet.

I wished I could advance to a more elevated spiritual state, without having to hurt any longer. With my eighteen years of age and with so much to discover ahead I noticed my sensitivity level was too acute to be able to achieve such demanding goals.

Everything appeared distorted before my eyes. I could not see beyond my fear of not accomplishing what I knew I was there to do: to serve others, to love, to live a wonderful and happy life full of inspiration. The pain seemed to grow increasingly stronger, nearly unbearable, and it was easy for me to escape out of it by inviting more drama, which was worsened by my suicidal thoughts. I had manifested the perfect image of Hell with my perception of the situation.

My depression became my everyday emotional state. I refused to accept my wonderful gifts because I thought I was wasting them on people who did not appreciate them.

I chose to go for a walk to avoid crying in the apartment, like I would find some answers on the street. The traffic chaos annoyed the pedestrians, who seemed to walk right through me as if I were a ghost. I felt my every footstep weighed tons. I felt myself to be a spirit with its body saturated with an unbearable heaviness and sorrow. I was in tears and nobody seemed to notice it, nobody would look me in the eye. I shuddered to know that there was no one waiting for me, no one to hold me at that moment. Everything was impossible to me in that existence. The sights of that beautiful afternoon seemed to conceal the sunlight and the color of the sky was getting darker, like announcing a storm was about to unleash. Everything around me, including my sensations, was blending in that darkness. I was contemplating the possible defeat before my cowardice.

I headed back to the apartment, opened the door and a few seconds later I was standing on my balcony of the fifth floor, ready to jump.

The suffocation grew stronger in my chest creating a very painful emptiness, and the pounding added to my despair. I looked at the sky and asked "Why is this happening to me? God, I don't care if I have to be born again and face this test all over again or quit existing, but I don't want to live anymore..."

At the very moment I was about to jump an unexpected force inside me had me stop. I crossed one of my legs to the outer side of the banister and I felt this force coming to the surface, bringing me a feeling of hope... suddenly a dazzling voice...was it my own spirit or the voice of God? It was telling me to calm down for a second and go back inside, where I could rest and avoid doing something tragic... I felt a miracle was about to take place.

I noticed the lightness of my being and I was soon floating in the air, watching my own body on the banister, ready to jump over. My vision had changed. I could clearly see the beauty of light particles connecting every tiny portion of space I was physically in. An Inter-dimensional door opened up in front of me, as if every particle, together with all the rest, was originating a beaming white-golden light.

"Hi!" I felt my soul speak without words.

"Am I dead?"

"Don't be afraid, I am your angel; I am here to guide you."

"But I'm outside my body. Am I dead?"

"As long as you don't deny me you'll be alive, and before you ask why, just let your feelings, your illusions and your dreams flow, in order to find out where you are, what you are doing, what you are looking for and what you expect. But you have to ignore your fear of yourself, of what you think is unknown, of ignorance. Imagine Paradise, just for a few seconds..."

These words echoed in my soul and they were similar to a poetic passage I had written years back. I could not understand what was going on, how could he mention these words that sounded so familiar to me?

"I am just translating your unpracticed knowledge..."

I clearly understood at that very moment that the communication between us was energetic. I could see light threads through which my energy blended with this powerful light, sharing bright white and golden rays. Our vibratory fields kept a luminous union where there was a clear light transference between us. That was what allowed the communication.

"What do you mean by "unpracticed"?"

"Wisdom comes with practice and I am reminding you that you have given up without having attempted using your true potential, your wonderful powers."

It seemed my guide was laughing with such a pure compassion that I felt like he was holding my soul.

"You have used one of your powers today, which is why I'm here--to remind you that you have powers. It is with your intention that you went through the density of what is visible and tangible and you opened up a door you call "inter-dimensional," through which you can talk to me."

Waves of light connected this bright being with my spirit, which slowly raised its vibrational frequency. I felt like we were holding each other but there was nothing touching my body, only these energetic bonds that blended with my floating being, a few meters away from my physical body.

"Are you my soul mate?"

"Your mind has chosen to identify its counterparts,

however we are several beings, physical and non-physical, that are in communion with you in this wonderful Universe."

"And how do I find you?"

"By taking care of your happiness with your ability to build bridges to love. The key is to use your talents, to establish bonds that put you at the service of consciousness awakening, to inspire those who need to come back to the Love that unites us all."

"How can I start?"

"Start by choosing which way to take, using the magic of your purpose..."

"But how?"

"Start by writing a book about this experience."

"A book?!"

"You will always be encouraged to keep your being upright, with your emotions in harmony with your purpose to open the doors to inspiration."

"So you will always be assisting me whenever I need you?"

"Yes, we will."

"But how am I going to prove to the world this really happened?"

He interrupted me wisely and said, "Open your eyes first, and get back inside. There is nothing to prove, just act from your potential. We will be answering as long as you connect with the powers that are asleep in you, the powers that every human being has..."

Suddenly, I saw the light floating away and my body just about to let go of the banister. I returned to my body through my chest, feeling it again and recovering my visual perspective. I sensed my consciousness was expanded; I felt sad but decisive that under no circumstance would I decide to kill myself. A miracle had happened. I slowly came back to the other side of the balcony and went back inside.

Tears started to fall down my cheeks until I burst into sobs and fell on the bed embracing myself, looking forward to rest. My crying went on for hours, until I got myself together and stated my intentions more clearly.

A new phase was beginning, with plenty of adventure and inspiration. I had no idea how I would take up this new journey of my soul. Neither did I understand what had just happened. An indescribable silence filled me with peace. I could see everything through different eyes, I felt more connected with everything around me. I went back to the balcony, this time to watch the sky, which was surprisingly clear and the first stars were already there. I knew perfectly that I would be guided by certain powers that I needed to awaken within me. I knew that the Universe had blessed me with a truth: we are all one, we are united by our purposes and we advance, together, towards their conscious fulfilment.

Thank you, Guidance. Thank you, Universe. Thank you, God.

1

The Power of Decision

Once you make a decision, the Universe conspires

to make it happen.

—Ralph Waldo Emerson

It is the practice of some habits and the unwillingness to change that clearly generate the circumstances you have attracted into your field of opportunities.

Here is the secret to opening your inner doors and using the powers within you. Are you ready?

~*~

Change your habits, and your life experience will change.

There is only one thing to take into consideration: decision.

~*~

You will not attract the things you really want at a certain point by continuing to do the things you have always done.

God does not choose favorites. This understanding will eliminate the belief of luck as a random circumstance in people's lives. It is the energy projected by our minds and emotions that shapes our reality in this cosmic field of infinite possibilities. Once you decide what you really want to achieve and you take action, the cosmic forces will join with you to fulfil your potential. Your choices and your actions will determine your "luck" factor. Your spirit is nurtured by love, all that is not love will only cloud your mind. The great news is, again, that you can always choose to feel better. That is a decision you have the power to make. Kahlil Gibran put it this way: "We choose our joys and sorrows long before we experience them."

There is a road to success in any enterprise, and it is encoded in the responsibility of being clear about what you want to experience. Your success depends upon your willingness to make headway in the direction of that particular goal, and to always decide to walk the extra mile to achieve it.

This is a way to transcend your limitations, to boost your feelings to a more confident state and restore your strength to take a firm stand towards your purpose of self-fulfilment. Be honest to your heart's desires, to your talents, and you will find divine happiness.

The following set of questions intends to help you

awaken your inner powers and return you to your natural state of love:

What are the things you normally do from the moment you wake up?

Do you follow a specific pattern and order in your everyday activities?

How would you describe your routine?

What is the most productive moment of your day? Why?

Who do you admire the most? Why?

Do the people you share your life with support your need to become the loving being you essentially are or to be successful even if that means changing your job or moving to another place or changing the activities you have been doing with them?

What kind of activities do you enjoy the most?

What would your perfect job be? Why?

Do you have a moment to clear up your mind and enjoy breathing during your day?

Do you have a moment to feel thankful for having opportunities to experience the infinite possibilities of this wonderful Universe?

There is something vital to understand in the journey to awaken your inner power and transform your life: if you do not love what you do from the moment you wake up, whatever that is, you are going backwards in the process of becoming who you really are.

It is by loving what you do, by feeling love and gratitude for this amazing life experience of yours that you are moving towards sacred guidance. Yes, you will be given the answers just because you have been asking for them with your thoughts and your willingness to change and transform your life experience. It is by doing this that you will start approaching your life choices with determination.

~*~

You will discover that only by loving what you do will you be in
perfect harmony to attract more loving things into your life.
You will invite the opportunities to accomplish your goals. You
have to feel love for what you do and your own determination
will bless your heart.

~*~

Are you ready now, to walk with determination towards your sense of mission? To become successful in everything you really want to do? To discover the divine and wonderful you? Are your ready to eliminate resentment, transcend your own limitations, and live your day passionately as if it were the last day of your entire life? Would you like to move in the direction of your dreams with clarity, to transform your thought pattern to become the alchemist of your own life? Would you like to return to who you really are—a loving being who wants to expand in this ever-expanding Universe?

Awaken your Power of Decision

You have attracted this book into your life because you are expanding your asking process. Guidance is being expressed back to you. Trust your desire; you are capable of being as happy as you have always wanted to be. You can start where you are right now, because now is the perfect moment. Overcome all types of excuses, for they come from your fears.

You just need to explore your heart's aspirations, your spiritual goals, and your sense of doing something out of the ordinary. Be honest with yourself, be clear about what you really want, and then enjoy the process of fulfilment.

Trust in your powers and in the divine guidance that will bless you whenever you open your heart and your mind with your calling. You are wonderful, compassionate, and beautiful; you are divine and powerful; you are love...

Enjoy your adventure.

Spiritual Workout 1

Explore the areas in your life that you consider to be in need of transformation. Trust your insights. Trust your inner-guidance that will bless your heart bringing you the activation of your power of decision. Surrender to your talents, to your loving intentions and you will achieve what you really desire. Contemplate this inner search for determination.

Spend a few minutes in silence, achieve the natural state of peace no thinking can break. Connect with the power of decision and envision your life transformation taking place at that moment.

Today, transcend the unproductive habits that interfere with this transformation you have dreamed for you.

Change the small things that fuel each old habit and invite the new habits that are in harmony with what your heart really wants. Enjoy your day. Nurture yourself doing the things that raise your well-being vibrations.

2

The Power of Forgiveness

The weak can never forgive. Forgiveness is the attribute of the
strong.
—Mahatma Gandhi

One of my inspirational teachers, Louise Hay, believes resentment is the cause of most health problems and resistance to change. Louise has transformed her own mind, freeing herself from her resentment and residual pain that she experienced after being sexually abused as a little girl. With her book and simple mantra, "You can heal your life," she can inspire us all.

You have the power of forgiveness and there is absolutely nothing you cannot forgive, because the power in you is greater than any situation that may have hurt you. If there is someone in your life against whom you hold a grudge, the sooner you relieve the unwanted pain, the stronger your power of forgiveness will become and the more prosperous and wealthy you will grow. Yes, you read that right. The sooner you forgive, the sooner you will become healthier and happier in every way. You have to believe you can. You have to act out of who you really are, a being full of love and compassion. Let the power of sacred guidance lead you to a place where you can heal the wounds in your heart. It is useless pouring salt on a wound and releasing extra emotional poison that will only contribute to causing an unbearable pain. You can heal your wounds by changing the way you think about yourself and those with whom you have a relationship—it is an opportunity to make a miracle. Whatever the situation you are going through, you can enlighten the darkness with your power of forgiveness.

~*~

Your ability to act from love and forgiveness will bless your experience, and will definitely begin to heal your life.

~*~

You can choose to delay this process by making excuses about why it is so hard for you to forgive. If so, just remember you can transform your actions with the power of your thinking. Your thoughts, if based on guilt or any judgmental belief, are a response from your perceptions of reality. While your wisdom is not belief-based, it just *is*, and it can only be *true* because it is connected with the divine essence in you, with your spirit, which you truly know by being naturally loving. How do you know this? Because you have practiced being loving and it feels perfect, like an eternal moment when you feel you are the closest to God. Can you remember those times you heard from your own or someone else's mouth: "Oh God! Oh my God! Oh God I love you..." "God this feels great..."? Most of these affirmations of sacred communion may have come from the act of sex, which is, for sure, one way to access divine proximity between two souls. An act that can co-create, conceive another body! But the soul cannot be conceived only because it was already created perfectly by God. If you accept this creation you are on your way to respecting the divine essence in every one you attract into your life experience. You can access the power of forgiveness easily when you recognize the limitations of your perception, and your thinking can be corrected.

It is in your ability to live right here and right now that you can be in communion with your spirit. By doing so, you can observe your judgmental behavior as another trap of your perception and you can, unquestionably, act upon what you know as the most wonderful response you can choose to give. You can choose to be forgiving.

The ancient Greek playwright Sophocles said, "One word frees us of all the weight and pain in life: That word is Love."

Once forgiveness takes place, a sense of joy and peace blesses your body allowing its exceptional response to heal every harmed cell. It is a natural process! You do not need to understand how your body does it, just trust in your ability to love yourself by having a positive attitude and the compassion necessary to forgive and let go. In practicing this, you will be able to get rid of the wounded personality, also known as the "victim personality."

You can also choose to blame others for the mental stagnation you have got yourself into. If feelings of blame are present you have the chance to bring awareness into your life by using your willpower. Your willingness is at stake here. First, recognize you can definitely do something about the way you feel and that you can choose to burn blame in the flame of your love.

Blame, of any kind, only invites resistance into your life and expands more pain all over your emotional and physical body. A mind with blaming thoughts can only perceive an unwanted reality, because such thoughts come from criticism, from fear and from a non-acceptance, an unwillingness to change. So, if this blaming comes to invade your mind, choose to observe without judging any of the circumstances. Just wait before you open your mouth to expand more of this unwanted, unhappy feeling and take a moment to shift from feelings of pain to better, more pleasant feelings. Practice detaching yourself from the judgmental behavior with the natural compassion you are capable of and you will experience a calm that is a manifestation of the inner peace of your spirit.

Listen for your inner voice, which knows how to guide you to surrender to the wonderful being you really are.

No matter what the circumstances, you have chosen to extend your suffering by focusing your attention on what happened, and it comes back to the present. In this state, you will be the only one who will be getting emotionally sick with your resistance to change, with your resistance to being resentment-free—to enjoying your unlimited ability to love. Your resistance to change and to forgiving is the only thing that can keep you away from your spiritual wealth. It is your thoughts and statements to yourself that can lead you to darkness. Light is always there ready to be reflected. That reflection will guide you to the wisdom of flowing in this magnificent Universe.

Nobody lacks will. Willpower, just like any other power, becomes stronger when it is used. Any idea of lack comes from fear, from the inability to act from within, the inability to be honest with yourself and to trust from your loving core. The mind is a wonderful tool, capable of translating the vibration of beliefs and feelings into intention and thought. This can only happen if you let it, by releasing resistance. It can also translate your spirit's divine energy, but you have to be willing to receive the translation. You know the phrase "lost in translation"? This happens not only with our spoken and written languages but also with our mental communication with our being. Your perception comes from your beliefs. That is why your mind needs training to be detached from unproductive beliefs. Any belief that is based in a lack of spiritual strength denotes fear. Any fear is unproductive if it is not used to recognize its emotional contribution to a given situation.

Your consciousness can expand when you change the thoughts that do not allow you to express yourself as a wonderful, loving being.

~*~

Your spirit is a source of infinite power, it does not believe in limitations or attachments. It simply *knows* and *is*.
It is free, and, as part of the divine source, it is pure love.

~*~

In everyday life there is always a guidance waking up your illusion of separateness. Dare to live every opportunity you attract in an open way in order to remove old habits and stubborn beliefs. Nothing happens by chance.

The Power of Forgiveness

~*~

Trust your ability to be fabulous:

an upright being with an unlimited power to love.

~*~

It does not matter how much emotional poison a person emits, you can shield yourself with a loving intention without engaging in combat, of which the only outcome would be more affliction and pain. We can certainly create a better communication by choosing the thoughts and words that match our intentions. Purity of words is possible; it means you are aware that words contain doses of energy and a thought pattern attached to them. Be careful with the way you use those powerful doses towards everyone you communicate with.

Set yourself free from your past and focus on *Now*. There is plenty you can do to reorganize your life and restore your natural state of peace and harmony. If you just let peace in you will feel much better. Remember you can always choose peace instead of resentment. It is your choice.

If you had an unsuccessful romantic relationship that you consider to have left you without the ability to love and to open up your heart to someone ever again, meditate more about this mindset you have decided to punish yourself with. There is no use in trying to hide yourself behind what you consider failure. There is no failure in life, only disappointment. In the process of starting to use your power of forgiveness you will discover that every relationship has been perfect to provide you with what you need to awake in you the most.

~*~

Results are simple answers to your way of reacting.
If you change your reactions, your results will change too!

~*~

Every one of your relationships was necessary for you to learn something about your power to attract. Do you think the people we relate to appear in our lives out of nowhere? There is more harmony than you can imagine in the field of possibilities. There are no accidents in the Universe, only the conception of them. Your emotional vibrations only manifest the possibilities you have attracted. Every single relationship is perfect for the vibrations you emit into the Universe. It can restore your awareness, taking you from illusion to love, to realizing how your signals are being expanded to walk confidently in the direction of your true purpose of having those relationships in your life.

You can spend your whole day cursing the people who you think have hurt you, but if you choose to do that I can assure you that you will only attract resistance to love, and you will remain in that state of pain. By living here and now, you release the emotional pain retained from past experiences, and you manifest the transmutation from fear to love, from pain to healing. In other words, you can initiate a miracle. To blame others for what you believe they did to you is a dense feeling based on the illusion that you are still living in that time and that they are separate from you. It is just another judgmental ego mechanism leading you to an unhealthy mind.

Everything is perfect. Dare exploring the eternal perfection you are blessed with. Stop blaming others for your own limitations. It is nobody's fault. Complaining about not having someone to love you will not help if you refuse to act lovingly. It will not help cursing others because you believe they criticize you all the time when you are criticizing yourself constantly. Start by stopping your self-criticism and respecting yourself more. You will see how easy it is then to respect others. Feng Shui educates us with the teaching that it is in our own house that we need to start.

~*~

You can heal your mind if you only release your resistance to love

by forgiving yourself and others.

~*~

Raise your emotional state to feel better; without blaming, just forgiving and manifesting, from now on, only the experiences you want to live. You can only live now, so why bother to pretend you are living in the past? Take responsibility for the way you feel, since no one else is responsible for "making" you feel that way. Only you are, by the way you choose to think. The great news is that there is absolutely nothing you cannot transform in your mind. Surrender to love. Any resistance can only bring illusion and fear.

If you are currently the target of an unwanted energy of violence or hate, recognize your energetic contribution to it first—the way you think, the way you interact, the way you communicate, the tone of your voice, your body posture, all that is produced by your emotions and your thought patterns—and then recognize your own source of love within, to open the doors for the manifestation of a miracle in your life. Apologize if someone feels offended by something you said or did, even if your intention was not to be offensive in any way. Apologize from your heart because in that moment you are being the loving, forgiving person you wish to be and you are allowing that same love and forgiveness into your experience. Even if the person chooses to remain offended after your sincere apology, you will know you have experienced the power of forgiveness within your own being.

~*~

The ego mind is responsible for any pain in your body, and it wants to be right. Your spirit, the sacred love source in you, only wants to be kind, to be compassionate, and to be forgiving.

~*~

Take a deep breath. Take some time to enjoy the silence, clear up your mind and release your resistance to love. There cannot be peace if you react with the same type of poisonous energy towards the person who shot first, even if this seems like the perfect justification. The way to bring automatic forgiveness is by choosing to stop attracting more drama into your life right there, when the opportunity for a miracle arrives. Choose to be kind. Act and treat others as you would like to be treated. You teach better with examples, and you learn better from them.

Here & Now

If you feel no one could give you the things you want for your life, feel grateful now, for you can go forward and provide them to yourself.

One of the secrets to success is to accept your goals, your wishes and decide what you want to develop in the process of achievement. If the way you act denotes the unwillingness to contribute a step closer to the realisation of your goals, then, review them, get inspired, and move passionately towards them. Make the most of every opportunity you attract into your life.

It does not matter what others think about you, only you can clarify your perception and enter the plane of awareness where you can easily find guidance. Whatever they think about you, or what you believe they think, has absolutely nothing to do with you, but with their way of perceiving reality. Each human being has their exclusive choice whether or not to live under the ego claws—criticizing and judging others because they have not found a way to transcend their own fears and act from a heart free from poisonous emotions. Trust your inner voice, which is wise and lacks pain, because its wisdom is based upon forgiveness, on the ability to love and to establish union with everything it connects with.

It is vital to achieve emotional balance, so always choose thoughts that generate well being instead of those that only lower your energy, making you vulnerable to external emotional imbalance. Any attack you feel coming towards you, you can transmute with instant forgiveness, starting now. You know that you are an eternal, indestructible being, when you feel safe and when there is no fear, only love.

The Power of Forgiveness

~*~

Wake up from the nightmare of pain and lack.

You are, essentially, compassionate.

You are a divine being with an absolute ability to love.

~*~

Use your past in a productive way. Learn from your mistakes and choose to move forward towards the next stage of your development. Do not get caught in the negative charge that certain memories can bring. Remember that if you are suffering for something that already happened you are not over it yet, meaning you did not forgive yourself or someone else. If you had not experienced what you have attracted into your life, you would not be who you are today, with the teachings those events may have awakened in you. You can change your way by looking into your past and learning more about the messages in each experience. Most of our suppositions about our experiences are based on our perception of the circumstances we have manifested. The best way for you to focus on your present is to move on towards your purpose and make the most of every opportunity *today*: to open yourself up to the power of forgiveness, connect to your inner peace, and receive the harmony of your sacred guidance.

Release your pain through forgiveness. True forgiveness is pain-free guaranteed. Maybe you have heard people saying to you, "What is done is done." But there is something deeper in you that perfectly knows that this is not as accurate. There is always something you can do. Start by changing the way you think about the "problem." Forgive yourself and the people involved, and invite the opportunity to eliminate pain from your past memories. Pain is an illusion at this moment. If you realize it is your resentment that keeps you attached to it, then release resentment by surrendering to your loving heart, by deciding to stop the war within your mind.

~*~

You are essentially love, and love can easily pass through the layers of resentment and blame.

You can forgive only if you let your soul express its true nature.

~*~

Ego-free Communication

If you communicate with true compassion you will not be thinking "You are an idiot," while you are shouting "Don't shout. I am speaking calmly." Harmonize your thoughts with your feelings in order to reach an ideal communication. If you think "My husband does not understand me," "I don't have enough," "My parents are too stubborn, there's nothing I can do," or "My sister wouldn't understand," you will have difficulties sharing your light with others, reaching your personal fulfilment, and communicating with your true spiritual voice.

Our emotional system warns us about the way we are manifesting our reality. If you seriously meditate upon the way you have lived your life until today, you will be able to find memories of a time when the reality you thought to be living turned out to be an illusion you had created. Pay attention to your emotions to predict where they are leading you.

Start your fulfilment by loving and respecting yourself as someone who wants to progress towards a higher consciousness. Nobody can give love without having loved himself or herself in the first place. Always leave space for surprises; nobody is so different than you, as you might think. Essentially, we all wish to be beings that live in harmony with consciousness opening.

The key is in the way beliefs can see only chaos where it can also be seeing love. For some unfortunate reason, many tend to be swept away by suppositions than can be translated to "It's not me, it's them!" "I didn't do anything wrong, they started to yell at me!" "They are all a bunch of idiots who are never going to change," "It's their fault," "It is useless to tell them, they will never understand." Ask yourself if these statements are based on a true living attitude towards your loved ones.

Are you giving yourself the space to learn something new out of this situation? Are you giving them the space to grow? Are you letting them express themselves with freedom? Can you visualize them harmoniously supporting your choices as you support theirs? Are you walking in their shoes, seeing life through their eyes?

Ask yourself what you can do from your heart, spirit, and mind to contribute to a significant change in all your relationships. What is important is not knowing who is right, but rather to cultivate the wisdom and the compassion of forgiving.

The truth in these situations requires much more than the suppositions that are only based on ego, on a separation from yourself and others. Do you think the truth is tough? It is up to you whether the "truth" is tough or not; it is your perception that makes it that way, as the concept of truth is based on your opinion, your beliefs.

If you choose to work from your ego you will continue to manifest the chaos that keeps so many people stuck in an unbearable drama. There is always a peaceful solution to each "problem" we believe we encounter. It is fully up to you whether you attract more drama or transform the situation with the wonderful radiation of your spirit. It is irrelevant to determine who started the fight; the important thing is to transmute it in order not to expand any more drama into this magnificent Universe.

Always remember, and this is not only a metaphor, that you can bring Light where there is only darkness. Saint Francis of Assisi inspires us with his wonderful poem that became his immaculate life devotion:

> Lord, make me an instrument of thy peace,
>
> Where there is hatred, let me sow love;
>
> Where there is injury, pardon;
>
> Where there is doubt, faith;
>
> Where there is despair, hope;
>
> Where there is darkness, light;
>
> Where there is sadness, joy;...

The writer Herman Hesse reminds us that it is difficult for human beings to sit down, take a moment to quiet the mind, and recognize that reality is not outside, but within us.

Spiritual Workout 2

Enjoy the silence. Take a moment today to sit and quiet down your mind to envision your perfect relationships. If you could only become aware of the amount of things you say and think everyday, you would spend more time in silence. You would wake up from the nightmare of poisonous communication and start living in the compassion plane.

Practice freedom from resentment remembering that it always takes forgiveness to heal any type of wound you think you have. Choose to set yourself free from any thought that leads you to blame.

Write a letter to the people who you feel wounded by. Be compassionate in the use of your words and forgive them. Keep in your mind the images of the things you love the most about them. That will help you raise your awareness and nurture loving intentions towards them. You may or may not choose to send the letter. It is in the act of writing it that forgiveness takes place within your heart.

Focus on your heart that beats without any conscious effort

from your mind. Breathe in and feel how wonderful it is to connect with your ego-free soul.

Release unwanted pain from past experiences, focusing on *now*. Ask for guidance, and you will be blessed with compassion. The Power of Forgiveness will heal your mind and body.

Look with your soul's lenses, instead of your physical eyes. Connect to the beauty in someone's eyes and embrace it. Say something beautiful to someone and change the subject when you notice poisonous statements. You will be surprised when you see how little effort it takes to reduce negative thoughts and drama in someone's heart.

3

The Power of Intention

We are formed and molded by our thoughts. Those whose minds
are shaped by selfless thoughts give joy when they speak or act.
Joy follows them like a shadow that never leaves them.
—Hindu Prince Gautama Siddharta

Every one of your thoughts contains a charge of your vibratory field. Your beliefs, your knowledge, your weaknesses, your insecurities, basically every feeling, are imprinted in that signal you send out in your thoughts. We are part of the universal consciousness and we have always related to it. That is why it is necessary to achieve your aspirations by focusing on your habits around them. If you really want something use your power of decision to transform the habits that are not in alignment with it, including old ideas, beliefs, and judgments. We all come from a divine source. By recognizing that, you are able to release the habit of negative thinking, of going against your own essence.

You open yourself to a world of possibilities just by thinking the way you do, obtaining the same frequencies you emit as a result. Buddha expressed it this way: "We are what we think. All that we are arises with our thoughts. With our thoughts, we make the world." Intend to feel better, to surpass your own limitations, to discover that God intended you as a perfect being, as someone ready to use all the potential you have been given. Intend, and then act.

Here is a simple way to call your power of intention into action: Be clear. Intend to live in alignment with your aspirations. Visualize in detail what you really want to achieve and act with the power of your purpose. Choose to have the thoughts that are in harmony with the kind of inspired life you want to live, and if you have thoughts that are not, exclude them completely.
Intend what it is that you would really like to attract. Make a list of your most priceless desires.

Here are some statements to help you brainstorm, choose, and manifest the best environment for healthy and prosperous relationships:

The Power of Intention

I am Free; therefore I use the power of my intention to express my divinity and I feel free following my heart's desires.

I am Love; therefore I intend to work with all my powers to have wonderful relationships, great communication, clarity and compassion with my partner, with my family and friends, and with everyone that I share precious moments with.

I am healthy; therefore I intend to be healthy by eating moderately, enjoying exercise, and having fun with my body that is the vehicle of my divine spirit.

I am happy; therefore my intention is only to attract people into my life I share mutual appreciation with, to be blessed by a cooperative attitude because we understand the importance of being loving, having fun, and enjoying our lives by feeling inspired.

I am inspired; therefore I intend to express my own divinity, my connection to the divine source, because it makes me happy to use my potential to inspire others to use their own.

~*~

Intend to live today being aware that every person you come
across is a reflection of God.

~*~

You are immeasurable; therefore, you can choose to live
your life like everything is a miracle, as Einstein put it. Do
those things you have always wanted to do, those things that
make you smile, that make other people smile, and that leave
your soul's print on the face of time. Intend devotedly to
attract what you desire the most. Here is the trick: be clear
about what you want the most, using the power of your
intention, imagine it is being played on a big screen in your
mind, trust your abilities to recognize what matches your
mental, emotional, and spiritual desires.

If you embrace that image for today, replacing every
negative thought that threatens to ruin the process of seeing
what you really want to see, with positive thoughts, then the
beauty of your clarity will be manifest in its full potential,
achieving one of the greatest goals in this age: to lift up your
mind with the power of your intention.

Releasing Judgmental Thoughts:

Making Space for Healthier Thoughts

You might have noticed the feeling you get every time you judge someone or something. Even if the conversation seems interesting you have to making up excuses for being judgmental by blaming it on your culture, your community, or the way you were raised, and start taking responsibility. Your thinking can be transformed because your spirit knows that it cannot be manipulated by anything or anyone, only your fear can produce an ego-driven response, when silence might be the greater one. Wayne Dyer says, "You can choose to be kind rather than being right."

It is your ego that always wants to be right. It is that idea that defines you as someone special by making someone else not! It is because of that belief that making someone wrong will always make you feel better. Do you really feel better just because you proved you are "right"?

Thoughts that bring emotions of anger, resentment, hate or any other similar lower mind-setting state cloud your potential. Even if you do not speak them out loud, thoughts emit negative signals. Transform your negative judgments into thoughts that bring positive vibrations. If you notice a negative judgment, from yourself or others, intend immediately to make a new positive statement that will easily invite the sacred guidance within you to take over. Transmute the negative into positive. This is possible because your own energetic system knows how to do it if you only have faith in yourself. It is easier to be kind, it is just in your memory that reacting from an "ego-mind" seemed to be the way to go.

A Course in Miracles inspired me with the idea that, "ego is an idea based in separation." Judgmental behavior comes from the response of ego's desire to be right. Your spirit knows better. To be loving is a choice as well.

~*~

Silence is necessary to quiet a noisy mind and connect with your spiritual potential. There is no need from your spirit to be right, nor to be judgmental because there is no separation between your spirit and God. Remember this and you will always have the chance to act from your intention to be peaceful.

~*~

Great-hearted intention can do miraculous things when manifested from your ability to think with clarity. Inner guidance will come to assist you always and only if you invite it in through your calling.

Choose the words you speak carefully. Do not hurt someone just because you feel hurt. If you feel hurt, admit it and deal with your wounds first. Free your body from them, releasing the emotional poison that hinders you in your way towards healthy relationships. Confucius said: "Forget injuries, never forget kindnesses."

Use the ability of your understanding to keep in mind that whenever someone hurts you, you are being invited to do a miracle. Once you act from your divine source you will realize you can be compassionate.

When you focus with the intention of being kind, the communication you desire will be manifested in your life, making it extremely difficult for those with negative judgmental thoughts to drain your energy. Be honest with yourself regarding your intentions. Exclude the words or thoughts that do not match your heart's desires and see those who are not clear about their intentions with true compassion.

Practice emotional detachment from outer opinions. Let everyone express his or her fears and insecurities without having that affect you. Do not let your ego dominate a situation by seeking to be right or to take control of a discussion. Everyone has his or her exclusive right to act stupidly, but that does not have to affect you. If the people around you keep on judging you, grow stronger and express with subtlety and true compassion your intention to be happy now, to have a meaningful conversation, to enjoy every single moment.

Only you can give ego the power to overcome spirit. Every unwanted experience is just another chance for you to connect to the divine source. If you knew you have the choice to alter your ego design, would you try? Of course, you would, and you can.

~*~

With every obstacle in my way I look up and sense the many millions of stars saying, "Hi."

~*~

Gossip has the effect of black magic. You can definitely hurt someone's energy if you talk negatively about him or her behind his or her back. Use "white magic" by sending love to people, by talking about their beautiful and loving attributes.[1] This is when the beauty of appreciation comes to enlighten us. This is something that you will be tested on everyday, because it is very common for most people to just ignore the fact that by talking bad behind someone's back they are hurting themselves as well. Misery loves company and judgmental people love to judge in groups—it is a way to have their negative opinions instantly validated by others. However, engaging in such a group is just another way to attract more drama into your life. The poison you are sending out expands and this affects your ability to connect with the ultimate meaning of your life, the path to peace and love, to kindness and compassion, to gratitude and prosperity. By losing part of

---

[1] "Black Magic" and "White Magic" are terms extracted from "The Four Agreements" by Don Miguel Ruiz, to describe the effect of positive and negative usage of words.

your energy in judging or gossiping, you are not connecting with the powerful messages that are constantly being sent to you.

Remember that by focusing on the light you are also sending light. Drama is there, ready to synchronize with anyone who matches its frequencies, but so is love and all the values you want to manifest in your life experience.

Every time you make a negative statement about yourself, or you gossip about another, or you say things that diminish you such as, "I am not good at this," rather than facing the challenge that is being presented to you, you are avoiding the power of your intention that can help you transcend limitations and overcome your fears. Maybe you are trying to learn something new that is very difficult for you, something you have never tried before. If you catch yourself repeating negative thoughts about yourself while you are learning, you are making it much more difficult for yourself to achieve that goal. For example, if you say that you are not capable of learning, this belief will expand. If you say, "I am so bad at that!" it will be very difficult for you to get better, even if you keep trying. You have already engraved it in stone. That is the influence of your thoughts that can only be transmuted by your powerful intention.

You already have everything you need inside you. Become the light that illuminates the source of your inspirations. Abundance is always manifested through the talents we have been given. Use the power of your intention wisely. Intend to live your life using the wisdom of your spirit and you will be amazed by it.

There is a Tao Te Ching quote that says, "Knowing others is intelligence; knowing yourself is true wisdom. Mastering others is strength; mastering yourself is true power. If you realize that you have enough, you are truly rich."

Falling Back into Drama

Most people are great masters of drama. The drama they create by saying and or thinking, *"This world is full of crap,"* or *"I don't care why things happen this way,"* or *"I hate my lif,e"* or *"I hate my job,"* or *"I don't have time to do what I really want to do,"* or *"It is his fault."* They have practiced it for so long that they have mastered it. They create the perfect scenarios that will allow them to live out their deepest fears—nightmares that involve worry, violence, pessimism, irony, hate, abuse. All of these feelings have one thing in common: they do not feel good.

Drama loves unwillingness, because it lives in fear. If you sit down and say, "I give up" and allow your will to surrender to negativity, you are letting drama take over. If you think, "I can't do this," "I'm too old," "I am not old enough," "I am not that smart," then you will be losing another chance to let the power of your intention surprise you with its force.

Imagine yourself using all that power of co-creation you currently use to manifest drama to create feelings of gratitude, love, and kindness instead—eventually, becoming a master of those higher energies. Every time you notice you are not getting what you want from someone, try sending love to that person instead of making the situation worse by hating something about him or her, which is a waste of your creative Qi.[2]

~*~

There is always something to learn in any opportunity of confusion, even from what appears to be unfortunate circumstances.

~*~

In order to avoid attracting drama, speak the language of forgiveness and acceptance, bringing a feeling of peace into your mind. It may be necessary to travel back in time, to discover the wounds that are still open in you, and close them one by one. It is an amazing journey to discover things you did not know about the way you were. The good news is you are not that person anymore and you can transform your life from now on.

You are full of love and that is the signature of your

---

[2] Creative Qi (also known as *Chi*): the artistic expression of vital and spiritual energy. It is the source of every idea that leads to a state of consciousness where enthusiasm flourishes.

creation. It is possible to act with compassion because you are full of it. Intend it and you will see its blessing.

If we spend our priceless energy of intention in living in fear and inaction, the beauty of life will be ignored and what we do not want will be all that we see, all that we focus on. We are here for a reason, you have used that inner knowledge many times until you got drawn back into drama and forgot the wonderful and meaningful adventure that you are capable of co-creating.

~*~

Take a deep breath now and meditate about the wisest secret to a magnificent life: to attract prosperity by being prosperous in your thoughts and feelings; to attract happiness by feeling happy; to attract love by loving yourself and others; to attract a friend by being friendly; to attract kindness by being kind; to attract health by making healthy choices and not introducing poisons of any kind into your body.

~*~

Think with joy and happiness embracing in your heart what you really want at this very moment... Now picture yourself being that, having that, feeling that way.

Spiritual Workout 3

Write a list of your heart's desires and the ways you intend to achieve them. Enjoy where your mind takes you while assessing where your soul is leading you.

Practice not judging your own actions or anyone else's.

Practice observing how poisonous thoughts can be transferred from one person to another through words. Stop contributing to that type of poisoning. Do not get involved in gossiping by intending to be aware of this damaging way of talking. Bring the seeds of compassion and a loving mind free from ego remarks.

Mind your own purpose and you will notice that just by focusing on who you essentially are nothing can affect you. You will be able to stop feeling offended. It is our sense of personal importance that feels attacked, not our true self. Nothing is against you; the Universe loves you.

Practice lowering the volume of your thoughts. It is possible that by doing this you will pay more attention to the silence, that is wise, on top of the deafening noise of most thoughts. A thought of peace and compassion requires the silencing of the rest of your thoughts.

Show your kindness in every opportunity. Do it for a whole day, even when you feel you have the right to break this wonderful principle, forget about right or wrong and just focus on your inner wisdom.

Keep in mind that you are spectacular; nobody can steal that from you. Live out your day according to this thought.

4

The Power of Purpose

Seek out that particular mental attribute which makes you feel most deeply and vitally alive, along with which comes the inner voice which says, "This is the real me," and when you have found that attitude, follow it.

—William James

You are the creator of your own fulfilment, absolutely nothing and nobody can separate you from your purpose. Therefore, every one of your experiences has been perfect for you to discover their messages today.

You are sharing your essence with the Universe's energy. Notice that every single event of your life responds to a pattern of thoughts and feelings. Accepting this will make your journey more pleasant and help you recognize the meaning "behind" your *coincidences*. In my spiritual ABCs *coincidence* is a synonym of *opportunity*.

There is no such a thing as "luck" in this perfect Universe, only the manifestation of your dreams which become realized based on your ability to act with purpose, or not.

Enjoy your path to happiness by already feeling joyful in the discovery of what you are attracting into your life experiences, since it is in this process that you are training your mind, transforming your consciousness, accepting guidance and emerging to the new era of thought where there are no limitations, only expressions of awareness.

You can start now, by recognizing your unquestionable desire to grow, to find inner peace in revealing yourself as you really are: a divine spirit having an experience in this physical, and, at the same time, non-physical dimension. In the middle of the 1920's the astronomer Edwin Hubble made one of the greatest contributions to science. He discovered that the stars and galaxies moved away from us and from one another. His conclusion was that the Universe is definitely expanding.

To help us understand, the Universe can be thought of as a balloon continuously being blown up. As a result the points on the surface of this balloon are moving away from each other. If these celestial bodies including our planet are in expansion, what effect does this expansion have on us as the micro cosmic beings of this Universe? In other words, think of the many ways the Universe is expressing its expansion. One of its expressions is you. You are a microcosmic energy body of this Universe, and you are expanding with it. Your flame grows and expands with each reflection of your divinity, with each act from your spirit. You want to be more because you desire to grow by expressing this divinity core that is one with the Universe. It is through our love-based intentions of giving ourselves to the flow of this Universe that we let go of our pain, frustration and scarcity.

Much of the drama and the pain people attract into their lives come from the beliefs that they cannot be inspired by their extraordinary purpose. This is caused by the opinion that inspiration is limited to particular or special moments in our lives. Making excuses to avoid showing our beautiful and loving selves does not contribute to the happy state of being present.

If you recognize that you want to be happy and prosperous, and you trust your talents, then you will awaken them by acceptance and practice. An "open mind" means, in this book, a transformation of consciousness, an expansion of your abilities. It implies the determination to overcome fear with the inner knowledge from your divine source.

Your thought frequencies, combined with the passion you add to those thoughts, creates your experiences.

Experience the pleasure of knowing and feeling, all the time, that in this wonderful life we can synchronize with everything we want to manifest.

James Redfield, author of the sensational book *The Celestine Prophecy*, wrote: "Knowing our personal mission further enhances the flow of mysterious coincidences as we are guided toward our destinies. First we have a question, then, we have dreams, daydreams, and intuitions that lead us toward the answers, which are usually provided to you through synchronicity, by the wisdom of another human being."

Are you committed to something completely unproductive? Do you feel happy with yourself, with what you are doing? Feel your talent. What is it? Imagine yourself using that talent as much as possible. Visualize it in your mind, feel it in your heart. Picture yourself having your time enhanced just by using that talent. Whatever your talent might be, stop reading now, take a deep breath and quiet your mind while exploring the beauty in that gift.

Ask yourself what you believe about that precious gift you have been given by your inner self, that part of you that connects with the sacred heart of every life form. This is another chance to discover what higher purpose is connected to your talents. Think about those beliefs that made you wait for better timing in your life to use your talents, and the excuses you used for postponing them. Each excuse for procrastination disables us from communing with the now and here, placing our attention in linear time (past or future).

Johann Wolfgang von Goethe once wrote: "A really great talent finds its happiness in execution."

Think about those agreements you made with yourself regarding when to use your talents and when not to. Are you saving them for a better occasion? Or maybe to impress that person you are expecting to appear in your life? Or do you only perform from your talents when there is nothing else on your mind and then, at the edge of boredom you say... "Yeah, now I'll do this because there's nothing else to do"?

Do not waste more of your precious life force!

~*~

Now is all you have. Your talents are the tools to build the dream of your life, to assist your soul's purpose in becoming one with other people's purposes.

~*~

Leo Buscaglia, renowned lecturer and best selling author of *Loving Each Other*, among other books, once wrote: "Your talent is God's gift to you. What you do with it is your gift back to God."

Meditate on this for a moment. What are you giving back to God? God is within you as well as in everyone, so your given power can be expressed all the time, by the way you think, feel, dream, and act. Every thought, feeling or action is your gift back to God. This is one of the ultimate secrets to success and happiness.

When you use your talents, doubts disappear. When you manifest your wonderful gifts there is no place for unhappiness. There is no such thing as loneliness when you play that instrument. There is a universal song that you are a part of and you are also the composer of one of its verses: your mission. Your verse is not small. It is as big and important as the rest of the verses. You will be hearing that song every day of your life because you are playing it in your soul, as well as in your mind.

This is the trick: match your purpose with your talents. They work better together. Whether you have a talent in the arts, music, communications, science, healing, use it with enthusiasm. The power of your intention will help you master your talents and you will enjoy every second when you are using them.

Dream on! Go ahead and spend some time envisioning the great life you deserve to have, while you use your wonderful talents with purpose. Vincent Van Gogh once said, "I dream my painting and then paint my dream."

Are there obstacles or blockages between your spirit and your talents? Are you procrastinating? If your answer is yes, then explore the limitations from your beliefs. Blockages are ideas that are made of laziness, procrastination, assumptions, pessimism, and attachments to unproductive habits among others. If you are sure you do not have any of what I just mentioned, then what you may have is a belief that is not letting you express what is within you!

The great Patanjali put it this way:

When you are inspired by some great purpose, some extraordinary project, all your thoughts break their bonds: Your mind transcends limitations, your consciousness expands in every direction, and you find yourself in a new, great, and wonderful world. Dormant forces, faculties and talents become alive, and you discover yourself to be a greater person by far than you ever dreamed yourself to be.

Your talents are an expression of your inner beauty that comes to life through your enthusiasm to manifest your purpose. When you are doing what you do well you feel enthusiastic because you are moving from routine to the magical role of co-creator. The passion you experience in this process raises your overall vibration field. To be living a life without using your talents is to be living without passion.

Here is an example of how your beliefs and feelings work to either help or hinder you in the expression of your talents and your purpose.

If your beliefs are based on some of these statements, "I do not have time to express my talent," "I am stressed out," "I'm too busy," "I feel too tired even to do what I love the most," then you are not expanding your consciousness; you are not aware of the meaning of feeling happy and living in harmony with yourself. You are accepting your choices in life, as they are the only ones you can choose from. This is another lie. You can choose better, way better, than that! Is it riskier? Is that what you fear—risk? What risk can be greater than living your life by fear and by doing the things you do not love doing?

~*~

Change the way you think, and follow the feeling that brings you into a state of connection and joy with your purpose and with your soul. In other words, find a way to enjoy everything you do by being present, by loving what you do, and this alone will be a healing experience to your mind.

~*~

Remember that your thoughts become your reality. If you are not satisfied with what you have been attracting into your life lately, if you do not feel good staying attached to your old beliefs, then change your mind-state! You can do it! But you cannot change the roots of those beliefs with the same perceptions that created them. It is necessary to transform your thinking by exploring the meaning of your present feelings. Your feelings alarm you about the quality of the choices you are making.

Here is a wonderful opportunity for you to do something amazing for your mind: *trust the wisdom in your spirit.* Feel enthusiastic and choose to change your thinking pattern under the influence of such a profound state of inspiration and, instantaneously, guidance will appear through an image, a voice within, a friend, a book, a knowing coming from your spirit awakening the power of your purpose.

~*~

It does not matter how big your dreams are. If they are reaching into the sky, you will need to build a stairway.

~*~

Intend to experience time in a different way. If your life is monopolized by your job and it is leaving you "no time" to express your talents, then transform your life! You can do it! The most difficult step is the first one, taking control of your habits and applying the necessary changes. Without change, your life cannot improve. You can learn to take the necessary steps to transform your current reality into one that supports your purpose. Use your time wisely. Invest it with integrity. Respect your goals only if they are building the pathway for you to expand your creativity and serve others in a greater way. Choose to invest your energy in expressing your talents more often. Regardless of what your talents are, just use them! Share them with the world. Your wonderful gifts can help others smile; feel joyful, healthier, organized, and inspired.

I like to use metaphors with music, because music has had a profound effect on my life. By no means are these metaphors intended to address you as a musician, singer or composer. Think about how many songs are not being written or played because those that have been blessed with the talents to create them refuse to do so. Listen to your inner muse and play the music you were meant to share, the music you feel most connected with.

You may wonder how you can discover the instrument you are meant to play, the one that is so particular that can only be played by you. This can be a job, a career, a service, etc. Well, there are many instruments that look alike, that are played by many people, but no one can play them in the same way, with the same message, intensity, and passion that you have. No one can play that instrument, write poetry, design computer programs—whatever your talent may be—with the quality and beauty that only you bring into your creative expressions.

Your mind and emotions respond to every vibration, and connect with melody or discord; it is entirely up to you!

~*~

Your talents are melodies that combined with other people's talents create a symphony. Work to find a tune with your talents and the talents of those around you.

~*~

Harmony is only possible when you express your powerful purpose in communion with the rest of the orchestra, when you add your tunes to the universal song. Ask yourself: what would the world be like without this collective symphony? War, violence, cruelty, and anger come from dissonance, from an unwillingness to play the tunes and train the mind to play harmoniously. This dissonance comes from the decision of avoiding rehearsals, of avoiding more practice, from believing that we are separated from "the rest" and from the unwillingness to be compassionate.

If you have doubts about this, then go explore history by yourself. Find out more about all composers, prophets, writers, and artists you are fond of, those who inspire you. Find out more about your guides, alive or dead, to get a reference point of what is being presented to you in this book. You could simply use all the names of the people I quote in this book. Are they aliens? How did they live their lives? And more importantly, what messages of guidance do they have to share with us? You will find that the one thing they all have in common is that they never surrendered to fear or became slaves to a job they did not really love doing, working only to earn money to pay the bills, eat, and, maybe, if time allowed, have some fun and use their talents.

We can get sick just by thinking about being someone we are not. Those great teachers are so respected because they stepped into this world and opened up the possibility for love, inner beauty, and unity for the next generations. They followed their dreams; they learned how to use their precious talents to master their lives; they used their gifts to build and inspire—to reach out and touch the hearts of millions like you and me.

Did they ever hesitate to share their talents with us? I am sure they did. However, they pursued their divine spiritual contribution and chose to live their lives with purpose to transmit their messages to us. It would have killed them not to share their talents with the world. You can choose to do the same. Express your inner music! Let it out!

We are not so different from them. We also have magnificent talents. Suppressing them contributes to the frequencies of insecurity, stress, depression, and unhappiness. No money can buy the talents that you have been blessed with; no one can steal them from you or express, better than yourself, the gift that only you can share. If you think it is possible for someone else to steal your ideas and do what you want to do, think again. This is not a competition; quite on the contrary, it is cooperation. If your talents are aligned with your purpose, the Universe opens up for you. You will attract into your life the right people who will be blessed by your contributions into the group plan we are all part of. In the process of consciousness expansion we are all one.

It is really up to you how you are going to bring your dreams to life. You just need to take action and use your talents. Do not wait until tomorrow; start doing it right now, even if you have to rearrange your schedule for today, or even if you are about to go to bed. Contemplate the plans you will put into action to start expressing your talent as you envision them. Einstein once said: "Imagination is everything. It is the preview of life's coming attractions."

To attract success we must be willing to transform our thinking patterns. If you practice something you love, more and more, you will definitely get better at it. Practice makes the master. A master is called a master because they have mastered their particular talent.

~*~

You will have to let go of stubborn beliefs and connect to the source of love in this magnificent Universe. You may even be required to de-construct your whole belief system and it will be worth it, as there is no feeling on earth like the satisfaction of living free from ego and limitations, discovering the true potential of your wonderful being.

~*~

Address your purpose. You already know there is a purpose for you to be here and now. Write your verse in the magnificent song of all times by contributing to the universal symphony.

Spiritual Workout 4

Write your *talent list*, and explain how each talent you possess relates to your mission, your calling, your heart's burning desire to serve, your purpose. Then create a 24-hour recipe to transform your mental barriers (your beliefs) that are somehow interfering with your purpose. Here you can create affirmations, meditation and visualization exercises, anything that you feel may help you be present and feel free from the resistance caused by any negative thought or habit. Write in another column your priorities in order, what you feel are the most important things in your life to be taking great care of. Explore your feelings while going through this process and meditate about what you can do *now* to achieve every goal listed.

Start manifesting your purpose by acting according to it. There will be plenty of chances for you to accomplish everything you are focusing your energy upon. Enjoy every moment while doing it.

Envision your perfect working situation, doing exactly what you love doing the most. Think about what you would love to share with humanity.

Find a spot in your house where you feel peaceful. Sit down, take some deep breaths and close your eyes. Intend to visualize yourself using each of these talents in communion with your purpose.

Read this list every day when you wake up and before you go to bed.

Explore the power of your talents by making use of them today.

~5~

The Power of Appreciation

Nature is full of genius, full of the divinity, so that not a
snowflake escapes its fashioning hand.
—Henry David Thoreau

Notice that the quality of your thinking depends exclusively on the way you focus your attention when it comes to your purpose. The farther the attention from your purpose, the greater the chances of having low vibrational thoughts. The closer your focus, the better you feel, instantly.

What would you like to achieve today? What can you do to enjoy every moment of this gift from eternity that we call 'today'?

You are a magnificent creation. We all are! Show some

more of your sincere appreciation to the service and the beauty of others. We all have a need for appreciation. It might make you blush to say something you appreciate in someone else. It does not cost you anything to share a few sincere words, but those words might cause the recipient to feel that boost of power inspiring their lives for years to come. You do not know what a clerk may be thinking, but you can certainly appreciate their eyes, their clothing, their smile, their hair, the service they provide, etc. If you express your connection with that person through appreciation you may contribute to increasing their enthusiasm to feel better. Moreover, it is a guarantee that you will always be welcomed with a smile. If you can focus upon what you like, rather than what you dislike, your power of appreciation will do the rest and bless your *today* with joy.

Appreciation connects you with the higher frequency of synergy (cooperation between souls to achieve something in a sublime way). It expands your awareness that there is love in everything and in everyone to be awakened. Every day could be a chance for you to improve this power only by putting it into practice. You can start by saying: "Thank you God, this is a great day, thank you for this opportunity to love again." Or, say whatever you want to say with sincere appreciation.

~*~

You know it will be a beautiful day, because you chose it to be that way. If you start each day with gratitude, it will be much simpler to have the mind state that allows you to think in alignment with what you essentially are, a loving and wonderful being.

~*~

The key to feeling better and discovering growth opportunities is using the power of appreciation. It is only by expressing your gratitude to every single contribution necessary for your expansion that you are in tune with the greater picture. Your happiness arises from that level of appreciation.

When you appreciate something your spiritual energy expands with the appreciated thing. We all have access to that power. Be aware and appreciate the simple fact that you can breathe, look at the sky, let the sunshine caress your face, feel the blessing of having another day to dream, plan, and move on your way with gratitude.

The possibility of using your appreciation power towards everything you relate to is exclusively in you because in each bond with your experiences there is a lesson that honors you.

Appreciate every day and experience without judging them. Be thankful for the knowledge they provide, even if you do not find a meaningful message at that moment. There is more wisdom in your life than you can imagine. It is totally up to you to have the power of appreciating everything that makes you grow and make headway in the path of personal freedom and fulfilment.

When you invest time in being in communion with the divine source, feeling grateful for everything you have and for the wonderful wisdom you can awaken to, guidance comes along to assist you in the process of fulfilment, raising your vibrations to those of happiness.

If you focus only on what you appreciate from others you will find the way of attracting the necessary peace to avoid the battles of ego and manipulation.

~*~

Every time you gratefully connect with your senses, your mind, your body and spirit, and you smile appreciating their importance, your immune system produces the necessary energy to keep you strong, healthy and dynamic.

~*~

Practice appreciation by adding feelings of joy and satisfaction to every situation in your daily life. Yesterday is gone and it is part of your personal history, it cannot condition your spiritual fulfilment. You are not the same person you were yesterday because you have already finished living that day. Judging yourself or others will not add any more knowledge for your next step in this adventure you have chosen. Try appreciating, instead of judging. Read the next question carefully and then meditate your answer truthfully (one that resonates with your spirit's wisdom). What would you rather do: judge what you dislike in someone or appreciate what you like?

There is nothing great in focusing on what we dislike. However, we can learn that if we do dislike something in someone, it is because we dislike that in ourselves. Start by acting in true line with what you really are, a powerful loving being by nature. Allow a sense of compassion to arise from your judgmental-free spirit, and observe the transformation in your thinking. The other person may continue to act the same way as before, but you will be a different person, feeling inspired and instantaneously moving by a transformation of focus.

Appreciate anything you feel grateful for, as tiny as it may seem. This is more constructive that any criticism towards yourself or others. Assume responsibility for your evolutionary process. Set yourself free from judging by under-powering your ego. We are here to give and receive talent and wisdom, to grow together, to enrich ourselves spiritually.

~*~

The smallest things that you are grateful for—like a glass of water, a piece of fruit or the food in your refrigerator—can remind of you how rich you are.

~*~

If you appreciate who you are, you are appreciating God, the Divine Source. Take a deep breath and appreciate the energy that nurtures not only your lungs but also every single organ that depends on that energetic transformation involved in your breathing. Nurture and respect yourself in order to learn how to nurture and respect others.

Appreciate that the Universe has a place for your desires to come true and is giving you the opportunity to experience it, to make it happen.

It might be a dog on the street that you can engage in a playful moment with, or the captivating energy of a painting or sculpture that raises your desire to express your own art, a stranger smiling at you that reminds you that you are sharing a wonderful world with everyone else, a pigeon eating the leftover bread crumbs of your sandwich, or a squirrel playing with its joyful squirrel partner, bringing you that laugh that can easily shift your thoughts to better ones.

You are attracting all of this into your visual field, but if you lower your energy level and allow depressing, angry, gloomy thoughts to take over your mind, all of this beauty will disappear from your sight and you will only see the things that match what you are focusing on.

~*~

Know yourself and you will receive a glimpse of heaven.
You just need to surrender to the miraculous flow of the Universe.

~*~

The Non-appreciating Mind State

The great philosopher Cicero once wrote, "Nature herself makes the wise man rich."

Use your amazing ability to see only what shines back at you through the natural world that surrounds you. Everything is surrounded by light, an aura that expands out from the physical form. Connect with all that shines around you, the sun, the moon, the stars, a stranger's eyes, a flower. There is so much beauty around and inside you, that if you would observe and connect with it you would be able to blend into the flow of this wave of *synchronicity*.

Thoreau once said that his profession was to find God in nature, which he did by retreating to a simple life in the woods, living off the land. He knew how powerful life force resonates from nature:

> I went to the woods because I wished to live deliberately, to front only the essential facts of life, and see if I could not learn what it had to teach, and not, when I came to die, discover that I had not lived. I did not wish to live what was not life, living is so dear; nor did I wish to practice resignation, unless it was quite necessary. I wanted to live deep and suck out all the marrow of life, to live so sturdily and Spartan-like as to put to rout all that was not life, to cut a

broad swath and shave close, to drive life into a corner, and reduce it to its lowest terms, and, if it proved to be mean, why then to get the whole and genuine meanness of it, and publish its meanness to the world; or if it were sublime, to know it by experience, and to be able to give a true account of it in my next excursion.

Spiritual Workout 5

Here is your first exercise to connect with your inner self:
Start your day with gratitude. Appreciate your body, your mind, your wonderful spiritual wisdom, your ability to enjoy this day connecting with everyone and everything you come across with. Feel the warmth and love from all that surrounds you blending with you.

Focus your attention on the world around you. Awaken the sparks of light in everyone with whom you come into contact. Share your sincere appreciation for their contributions to your experience on this planet, always remembering that everything is perfect around you. Trust in your power to appreciate each opportunity and you will certainly inspire the best out of it.

Volunteer in something that makes you feel great and enjoy experiencing the power of appreciation as you do kind things for someone in need.

Get in the habit of saying, from your heart, "Thank you, you are very kind." Sincerely remind people that you are aware of their contributions.

Practice paying sincere compliments to raise someone else's energy. Express your compliments from your heart while you are acknowledge what you like about each person you meet. It might be the color of their shirt, their eyes, their smile, their voice, their hair, their ideas, their enthusiasm, and their beauty in general.

Appreciate your health: wake up to a pleasant piece of music, respect your body at the gym, eat healthy food, and close your eyes and think of something relaxing when you have stressful thoughts. Remember that stress comes from a pattern of thought, and you can always change the way you think.

~6~

The Power of Will

Do the thing we fear, and death of fear is certain.
—Ralph Waldo Emerson

The only thing that can stop you in this Universe is your own fears, but fears can be big motivations to grow stronger. If we let fear become intimidating, hope can become weak and your willpower might not manifest. If fear becomes your basic emotion, and your doubts get stronger, your perception of the environment dimensions will be altered. The way you perceive reality depends on the way you hold on to your belief system.

We cannot change others, but we can study ourselves to recognize our own fears and use them to our own self-improvement. All emotions gain power with our every thought.

It does not matter if you wake up "thinking positive" and you go to bed the same way when your feelings do not match that positive mood. It is your emotions that together with your thoughts determine your state of connection with the Universe. It is useless to say: "I think positive," if that statement is in fact hiding lots of doubts and fears that you do not want to face. You have to find the message behind your lack of self-confidence.

Doubts and fears can definitely be useful to find the way to be prepared for anything we need to develop. The more fears and doubts you have, the more opportunities you will have to overcome them. If you invest your energy in observing the way in which fears harass you, every time you feel invaded by images, thoughts and disturbing emotions, you will expand your field of attraction over the infinite possibilities to transcend them. Remember your spirit needs to enrich from the environment's energy to keep calm and emotional balance.

Grasp a beautiful image in your memory to be able to realize how your emotions affect your environment. Whenever you are conditioned and limited by your own beliefs filled with drama, you have to step outside that dense circle and connect to the energy of something beautiful that can counteract, to be able to attract a new and wider view.

We have to be very careful and pay attention because it is easy to lose focus when you miss an opportunity because you allow your doubts to seize you, lowering your energy to dense vibrations of disconnection to the divine flow of the Universe.

If you work to discover your own denial mechanisms you will find the way to face your fears, to live in peace with everything that surrounds you. As long as you know what you want, you will know what you need. You will be able to eliminate the idea of failure and doubts, because you will trust that everything occurs according to the opportunities you keep attracting, to develop your potential. In using the power of your thought you change your way of understanding your fears and you decide to overcome them; your willpower will be ready, as long as you let it flow. Fears can motivate you to go beyond your own self-imposed barriers. Use them as fuel to activate your willpower and achieve your self-fulfilment as the capable being that you are. Increase your self-esteem and your self-confidence—which are so necessary to manifest your purpose—by facing your fears.

There is a great story about my mother and me that can be applied to show how fear can be useful to develop courage. I grew up in a village by a big river. My mom, though, is afraid of the river. She never learned how to swim and my grandmother shared the same fear. Since she was a child, my mother could never convince herself to learn how to swim, instead she would say: "I respect the river."

I can still hear her voice telling me as a kid, "Stay where I can see you! Don't let the water go higher than your chest." She projected her fears onto me and I ended up sharing her fear of the river. By age fourteen I tried taking swimming lessons, but, as expected, my fears were still too powerful. I gave up the lessons and realizing that I was facing my own limitations. I chose to change my thoughts and asked for help from the bottom of my heart, some kind of direction to be able to control my fear of drowning. Days after that, I was inspired while watching a movie. A beautiful message drew my attention: "If every time you find something that you fear, you face it, you will more likely overcome it." In lieu of my current fears, I felt like this message was addressed especially to me. I knew that I just had to face my fears.

We all know that it is easier said than done. When the movie ended, and without paying attention to my doubts that were still alive, but incapable of defeating my will, I ran to the park that was at the river's edge. The shadows of the night seemed to move gloomily; the clock was nearly striking midnight and the silence was playing a challenging melody.

I took the idea of conquering my fears very seriously, my fear of loneliness, the dark night, the challenging river. I jumped and started paddling with my arms until I was definitely swimming. I could not see the coast or where I was headed. Ten minutes or so went by (which felt like an eternity) and suddenly I bumped into something with a mysterious shape and density. I was horrified. I swam faster than a world champion and I was on the coast probably two minutes later. I thought to myself, "I really respect the river."

During the following weeks the midnight dip became part of my routine. The river and I found mutual admiration. I even started to enjoy the beauty of the moon reflecting on the water, the mystery of the things in the water that my body would bump into and the pleasure of understanding I had faced a great challenge—maybe even one involving an unpleasant memory from a former life.

I did not give up connecting with fear, with the deep silence of the night and the water, with the scary shadows in the coast and the things I found in my way, I am still unsure if they were floating branches or strange creatures. But it was me who had changed. It was my intention that had manifested. I mixed myself up with the river's spirit. I gave myself up to it, and respected each particle because I knew that was the only way to overcome my fear, to face it with my will.

What I still did not get back then is that I was going to attract bigger and more important challenges into my life and that I would have to face other fears that I did not even know I would have. Believe me: I am sure I nearly drowned one of those nights!

Productive Fears

In each challenge lies the gift of self-knowledge and self-consciousness with which we are blessed when the moment arrives. The beauty in this is that it does not matter what you are afraid of, you can use and transform your fear into what I call a "productive fear."

Where there is a state of fear, there is also a state of transcendental consciousness that produces a parallel feeling of calm. It is all right to be afraid; our organic and energetic system always warns us about a potential danger. Fear prepares the body for action. Initially it can be thought that some fears come from energetic wear and tear and from an imagination structure based on ideas of being on the defensive, given that it is possible that fears lead to weakness, attracting helplessness feelings. If one educates oneself spiritual and physically, then one understands that each of those fears is introduced by your emotional system to be faced instead of ignored. To alarm us on the existence of a discrepancy between what we want to attract and what we are actually attracting, there is no ignorance in the absolute awakening consciousness: only the fulfilment of the bodies we form in search of unity.

If you are going to a job interview and you feel uncomfortable and anxious, ask yourself: "What am I thinking? Why am I giving power to someone that is behind a desk letting myself lose my self-confidence?" These are alarms of your own fears about the possible fact that you are not well prepared for the interview. It would be really useless not taking the opportunity to attract a higher vibrating state and face the fear to increase your self-confidence level. Only that way confidence will take the most important place at the interview that has not yet happened, and you will be able to attract what you consider success and discard what you consider failure.

Each fear is productive because it gives you the opportunity of activating your self-confidence and developing your will. You have the power of doing whatever you really aim to do. You have the will of dispelling any fear that appears. The only thing that stops you is your own resistance to change. The overcoming of your fears is only possible by taking responsibility, as it is you who give them power over your actions. Whatever it is you want to do, do it today. When the opportunity arrives, answer the call. Allow the experience to enter your field of attraction fully.

Do something you want to do but you are afraid of. Remember that you are always attracting the opportunities you need the most to overcome those attitudes you have used throughout your life as barriers against accomplishing your personal and spiritual development. When you are determined to face your fears, you will get to understand their essence, which have their roots in your own imagination. All you imagine can lead you to strengthen your courage; therefore, do not let yourself be swept away by pessimism. On the contrary, use your willpower and trust yourself and the divine guides that you have found along your way—even if you are just awakening to the fact that they exist. One big learning opportunity is through experiencing what you fear the most.

Try to connect to the main source, with the higher frequencies of consciousness. Be aware that your fear is there to teach you something. Each fear you experience, you have attracted into your own life to learn more about your willpower and your ability to reach your goals. Use your energy to listen to your doubts and answer that you are safe, convinced of what you really want, and ready to get that job or start that relationship or to move to another country. Laugh at yourself, at your fears. Go to the mirror and transform that fear into a funny face, and laugh a little bit more, until you feel better.

Every time you are afraid of something sit down and do what I call a "smart search" until you discover the thought that gives you the security and feeling of confidence you need to gain control of the situation. Remember always that what you think, as well as what you fear, manifests.

If you are afraid of loving someone because you think that once you did and you "lost" that person, you will continue to attract the same experience over and over again until you discover that that is not love. True love does not have limits. Love that leaves you feeling exhausted is not real love but the illusion of love. Being reluctant to truly love, you are attracting disappointment, drama, and more fear because you have avoided using the power of your thoughts to change your ideas about your concept of the "love" you are referring to. Change your attention and fear will turn into a cause to attract that relationship and to be able to, with your willpower, grow loving.

The only way for us to understand the message hidden

in our fears is in facing them. Talk to them. Look at the imaginary world behind them. See everything as if you were out of your body and then use your willpower to get ready to conquer your feeling of inability. Do whatever works for you, but face them and get rid of them!

Be aware of your own mental barriers and imagined limits. Once you notice your own reluctance to accomplish your goals, you will have the opportunity to make a different choice, act with enthusiasm, change the way you do things using the power of your will.

If you still feel your actions are being poisoned by fear and your inability to act has taken control again, take a moment to rest, take a deep breath, and relax as much as you can.

Remember all the powers you possess. Connect back to everything that shines around you and decide you will proceed from your will. Because deciding not to use the lessons that your fears can give you would be to waste you potential to make headway towards the life you want to live.

Spiritual Workout 6

Remember that in the roots of your beliefs there are the barriers that have conditioned your wonderful potential. If you change your beliefs and your thoughts when they are poisoned with lies you will be able to use your willpower easily and discover how privileged you are.

Exercise your willpower by doing NOW those things you have always wanted to do but procrastinated with excuses. There is always a course of action you can take to overcome your fears and address your most important goals. Do what you must do to take action, one action at a time, facing each fear as it comes up and conquering it as you go.

You can also close your eyes and imagine the barrier between you and your goals. Imagine yourself transforming that barrier into a ladder and starting to climb it.

Break up with illusion and apply the technique of getting ready for action. Prepare yourself mentally, spiritually, and emotionally the best way you can. When you feel ready, act!

Use your fears! Let them push you towards growing stronger and wiser.

The Power of Passion

The happiness of a man in this life does not consist in the
absence but in the mastery of his passions.
—Alfred, Lord Tennyson

Remember that popular saying they used to teach us as kids, "Why leave for tomorrow what could be done today?" Start your self-fulfilment by living and respecting yourself as a human being who wants to move forward towards a higher consciousness today.

Do not leave for tomorrow what you can do today. Every time you procrastinate you miss the opportunity to find the wonders of life, to access a whole world of possibilities for you to feel the happiness you have always wanted. You will begin to attract the opportunities to enjoy life as soon as you decide to detach from outcome and start feeling enthusiastic in every second of your present moment. Carpe Diem! Seize the day and do not procrastinate. Now is all you have.

When you realize that there is no need to seek the approval of others, you will naturally detach from the outcome and enjoy every moment of the experience of sharing without expecting any rewards. The reward is already with you the minute you express your true purpose.

Just by experiencing the joy you feel when you express your gifts you are already attracting what your soul really wants. Just by breaking away from the outcome you are fulfilling part of your purpose. We are a mix of strong passions, so that one second of feeling like a failure could obscure our whole vision. That is how someone can get into the low frequency that will only attract similar frequencies. It is the way we feel that keeps the signals expanding, attracting. If you want to have a wonderful experience today, do not diminish your energy; do not poison your co-creative power by focusing on the things you do not want. Do not contradict yourself by sending the wrong messages. Be clear and trust your values and your purpose in order to be blessed with any experience you wish to attract. Feel great about it. It is all about passion!

In the wise Toltec philosophy the Death Angel is the one that is always around us, working by our side, teaching us how to appreciate life.

Death has already won the game; it is not necessary that you struggle against it. The Death Angel is always teaching us that when the transition moment arrives he will be ready to guide us. We can take absolutely nothing material on that journey, just the energies of our vibrational field. Therefore, it is important to have prosperous relationships, in which we give the best of ourselves, to make each step that we take another step towards our self-fulfilment and in which our energies produce vibrations increasingly more in line with our purpose.

The wisdom behind this angel must not be ignored. Fearing death is natural, as long as we notice that this fear will cease once we start enjoying every day and expressing ourselves in the best possible way towards everything that surrounds us. Here is the key to living a life full of enthusiasm: Decide what you really want to do. Explore yourself:

What are the things you always wanted to do?

What do you enjoy doing the most?

What kinds of activities have you stopped doing and have always regretted?

You cannot attract love by doing things you do not love. Decide what you want to attract into your life and start living it. Start doing it with all your heart and body. Call for guidance and observe what happens around and within you. You will be given the answer that will lead you to invite your power of passion and go wherever you want to go with your talents.

If you always wanted to learn how to play an instrument, what are you waiting for? Start manifesting it now by enjoying the feeling of seeing yourself doing it. There is a great power in the art of visualization. Believe you can achieve this goal.

If you always wanted to express your creativity doing something artistic, start manifesting it now by taking some lessons. You will only be able to make it by trusting your abilities and believing that there are no barriers other than the ones created by your own beliefs and emotions.

Your talents should not be given up; they should not be left inactive. It all depends on your taking the decision without ignoring your *Death Angel* who is always encouraging you not to abandon your purpose. Each day that goes by without you doing it, is one more day you are missing the magnificent chance of making your soul shine, of becoming the alchemist of your own life, of experiencing your self-fulfilment.

This transcendental teaching helps us manifest our gifts naturally and easily from an early age, so we can transcend our own limitations and make progress in the use of our talents.

Enthusiasm is the key to manifesting your ultimate dreams. If you focus on living passionately you will learn to enjoy everything that surrounds you and transcend the attachment to your possessions.

~*~

Passion guides you to live your life in harmony.
Nobody can forbid you to enjoy that sacred feeling inside you,
whatever your goal is.
Visualize it happening at this very moment.
Use your senses to manifest the sensation of living your dream.
Keep your vision, make an effort to hold on to it, and most
importantly, smile as if you had already achieved it.

~*~

Passion is necessary in each enterprise to accomplish what we need in order to grow spiritually.

You are challenging your potential with every step and every experience you attract into your life. Your talents will become stronger as you make use of them. By changing old habits you will be able to awaken your creative potential and start enjoying your life with passion. Challenge your routine and you will discover that practice makes the master. Exercise your creative power and you will expand your talent by attracting serendipity into your life adventure.

If you put off until tomorrow something that you have the ability of accomplishing today, there are high possibilities that you will regret it. Whereas, if you make the most of every moment, it is not likely that you will spend energy in thinking about what you could not accomplish, given that you have already tried the best use of your powers, and if you did it with passion, then you will feel completely satisfied and will have taken very good profit from your whole life experience.

What you strive for every day is the response to the interaction between what you feel and the way that feeling creates your reality. Your perceptions can be limited by your feelings. In order to raise your perception level in a wide and bright way focus on the sunlight and the many stars you are able to see. This can easily give you a perspective of the infinite source. Allow the images to bring the beauty to you and to everything that surrounds you, and *carpe diem*!

It is invaluable to be able to do what we desire when we want to with freedom and without feelings of obligation. NOW is the key to tomorrow, but tomorrow is another range of possibilities. How different would this world be if you were just able to live every day with passion? You would discover how much there is to do, how precious a day is and how wonderful it is to fully enjoy it. At the end of each day, when the moment of meditation has come, all that has been done will delight you and you would have the perfect opening for a restful sleep instead of worrying about what could have been done. Most of all, you will envision the day to come and its amazing opportunities with great enthusiasm.

Nothing can divert you from your inner path, unless

you allow it. You are responsible for any deflection. Remember meaningless accidents do not exist. Every accident teaches us something related to change.

You are the director of your movie, your adventure, and only you can choose whom to share it with. Spread your passion for what you do to others, share your smile, and remain focused on the experiences that lead you to create something new.

Remain strong and trust your spiritual and physical path. Inspiration comes when we let our purpose guide the way. Passion and spirit is the perfect recipe to develop your purpose.

The magic of using your talents will lead you to inspire others, and, when you least expect it, the people you interact with will be vibrating in similar frequencies of spiritual communion with you. You will be able to see that many people feel happy about having attracted the successful experience of sharing their talents with you. You will realize that teamwork generates higher levels of consciousness. Michael Jordan said, "Talent wins games, but teamwork and intelligence win championships." Apply this to every relationship you have.

Spiritual Workout 7

Start your day with a big smile, feeling grateful for everything you are, and all you possess. Say out loud from the moment you get up, "Today I am feeling enthusiastic about this beautiful day. I am investing my energy in raising my feelings of joy and happiness. This is a perfect day! I am living my passion!"

Connect with your inner creative power. Feel your talents and express them as much as you can. Go and study what you really want to learn. Explore the resources of this amazing Universe.

Get detached from outer opinions. Nobody else is responsible for your actions. Choose to trust yourself and act in line with your purpose. No one can weaken you unless you allow.

~8~

The Power of Beauty

It is difficult to say what is impossible, for the dream of yesterday

is the hope of today and the reality of tomorrow.

—*Robert H. Goddard*

Our nature is one with the Universe. Accept the beautiful cosmos as part of our own little cosmos inside our bodies. We are the Universe, in miniature.

The shining energy of the life force is reflected in the beauty of all that already exists. Be grateful for this beauty and invite it into your life. Nature is an expression of God's design and it is there to nurture you.

If you want to experience love and compassion, you have to become loving and compassionate. When you complain about being overweight or too skinny or not having the right type of nose or the desired muscle mass you are ignoring your inner beauty.

Beauty can only be achieved by bringing your inner beauty alive. Thoughts that lead you to compare yourself with others in terms of physical beauty are thoughts you cannot afford to have because they will deplete your energy and will prevent you from focusing on the wonderful being that you are.

Start by changing the way you address your body, since it is not separate from your mind at all. As you think, you become. You create your reality with your every thought.

By loving yourself you will attract the opportunities to nurture your body with a healthy lifestyle. You will understand the importance of enjoying a daily workout and eating moderately and happily. The quality of your thinking is the key. If you change the way you have always thought about your body, your physical image will change to your own eyes. It is that simple. Thus, it requires a type of attention that invites the feeling, "I am beautiful" as the secret ingredient. Be aware of the loving and beautiful being you are, and share it.

Even if you cannot see beauty in someone, it is always there, because beauty is within us all. Some people may say they have trouble seeing beauty in you, but you are still beautiful, regardless of outer opinions. To be detached from people's opinions is a wonderful and necessary daily practice on your path towards your inner and beautiful self. Self-confidence is a major step in developing a healthy lifestyle. You do not need anyone to tell you how beautiful you are because you already know it, and because if you keep asking others for approval you are depending on their opinions for your happiness. If they think you do not look so good and you believe it then your ability to love yourself will be affected. As one of my most important teachers, Wayne Dyer often reminds us, "Become independent of the good opinion of other people." Accept the path of self-confidence and trust your inner guidance about what dress to wear, what shirt to use, what hair cut looks better on you or what color will boost your mood when you wear it. "But, blah blah blah..." There are no *buts,* no excuses that can bring down your amazing power of beauty, only by following your intuition can you transcend the old habits of not nurturing yourself with loving thoughts, feelings, and a healthy lifestyle. You are going to have lots of fun if you trust your inner guidance in this. If you start loving yourself, your beauty will radiate out its true power.

Be a Pro-solutionist

You can probably remember some experiences when something someone did or said hurt you badly, or when you felt that someone had stolen your energy by placing your attention on what you did not like about them, or when someone tried to poison your energy field by judging you. You will be repeatedly tested by your own power of attraction, until you have mastered the art of minding your own purpose, and allowing others to have their opinions without defending yours as the only one that matters.

Work on replacing the idea of "bad luck" with the idea of "opportunity." There is no place for bad luck in this perfect Universe. Choose to have thoughts that connect you to your inner beauty rather than those that connect you to a feeling of *"I'm a victim, and this is my collection of memories to prove it."* Reach for the thoughts that bring you peace rather than the ones that alter your vibrational field leading you to the basement of your unwanted self, to the personality you have developed to protect yourself when someone puts a finger in a wound you have left unhealed.

When someone tells you something you find offensive, unravel your belief system to find what belief is interfering with your ability to foster peace rather than blame towards that person. I know that nobody wants to take responsibility for the actions of others, so we should stop believing we can change people's actions. Choose to focus on the solution rather than engaging in the circumstances that you do not want in your life experience.

If you are what I call a *pro-solutionist* you are focusing only on solutions and all so-called problems cease to exist. The historically designed ego has taught us for generations that we are better or more special than others. Break the bonds between your own beliefs and this design. Transform its shape until ego becomes a simple idea that will only visit you again when things are not happening the way you want them to, bringing you again the opportunity to focus only on your purpose, which is always sacred. You can become your own sculptor, shaping your own life, and bringing out the inner beauty that was hiding in the core of what initially appeared to the ego mind as an obstacle.

Nobody can offend you unless you have invited that situation into your creative experience with the resistance to being loving, to accepting the solution rather than the problem. Nearly everyday we have the chance to transform, just like an alchemist, any material into gold, any feeling or situation into beauty. If you act from beauty, you will see beauty reflecting back at you.

When you are driving and someone cuts you off in a violent way, you may send that person lots of nasty thoughts, and you might even hold onto your angry thoughts until you get home and release your negativity with your spouse or children. Then the next day it happens again and you begin to see that there is a pattern in you that presents you an opportunity for a change, a chance for you to understand and practice the connection with everyone and everything around you without taking anything personally.

Nobody has the power to offend you; it is you who feels

offended and gives power away. Even when extreme violence takes place it is not against you but only a reflection of what is being manifested from someone else's lower energy fields. Nothing is really about you. Mahatma Gandhi once said, "Whenever you are confronted with an opponent conquer him with love."

Connect with your spirit; observe how good it feels to act with love and compassion; think about the beauty in your coincidences, and focus on all the wonderful things you can do for the people you have invited into your horizon. Think about your talents and hold on to that thought. Think about something you can do to make others feel good, such as listening, playing a song, hugging or being a helpful friend. Smile to yourself. Nobody can stop you from expressing your own powerful nature.

~*~

There is a land of beauty to be discovered in all of us. Intend everyday to explore the beauty of those around you and inspire them to express it.

~*~

If you are thinking that you are full of sadness or worries, dig deep inside, and you will find that there is also the power of forgiveness to help you release any resentment and bless you with joy and inspiration. Pay more attention to your own beauty because, like it or not, you will manifest your feelings and opinions in your body and your actions. The way you feel about yourself will condition all your experiences.

Connecting with your inner beauty can shift your thoughts away from feelings of ugliness to feelings of love. There is love in you, and being in touch with it will transform your vibrational field. You will start to feel safe and this feeling of safety will transform your energy to help you grow to be more hopeful and receptive. The secret to beauty is to engage in the habits of self-confidence. It is through this that you move towards loving yourself, to an amazing state of co-creation where beauty is manifested physically, emotionally, and spiritually. Goethe once wrote: "As soon as you trust yourself, you will know how to live."

There is so much beauty around and inside you that if you observe and connect to it you will receive the necessary energy to be able to take a deep breath and return to love, your natural state of well being.

Spiritual Workout 8

Show your beauty by acting beautifully. Be aware of the loving and beautiful being you are, and share it. If you act from beauty, you will see beauty reflecting back at you.

Trust in the power of beauty within by being independent from the comments and opinions of others. Discover the way you think about yourself—are you beautiful? Of course, you are. Are you acting beautifully? Maybe not yet. Intend and be clear about the changes you consider necessary to introduce this week to transform your lifestyle into a well-being plan of manifesting your beauty from the inside out. Write down the affirmations about the changes you are already visualizing regarding your goal of becoming a confident, independent from outer opinions, and beautiful being.

Give more of your energy and beauty when listening to a friend, spending time with your family, sharing a great story with someone, or helping a co-worker.

Observe anywhere and anything and you will find beauty, and recognize a reflection of yourself in it.

The Power of Love

Freedom and love go together. Love is not a reaction. If I love
you because you love me, that is mere trade, a thing to be bought
in the market; it is not love. To love is not to ask anything in
return, not even to feel that you are giving something—and it is
only such love that can know freedom.

—*Jiddu Krishnamurti*

Are you aware of the power of your soul? We are not less important than the energy source that originates the brightest stars. The greatest knowledge of all is that only through the eternal search for truth do we find the way to the inner source of what already is, love. What is love? Can you describe it? Yes, but once described with words its transcendental meaning gets distorted. Love can only be experienced by loving. Thousands of poets have tried to explain it, and their only success at doing it was their discovering of how unnameable love is. Our essence is shaped in eternity and blends in unity. Separation only comes from ideas, limitations, unawareness, and fear.

A Course in Miracles reminds us there are only two emotions: fear and love, "All fear is past, and only love is here."

In a translation of the ancient Hindu text, the Bhagavad-Gita, Krishna (*the divine one)* explains to the Master Archer Arjuna (*the bright one*) the transcendental importance of the spirit: "The working senses are superior to dull matter; mind is higher than the senses; intelligence is still higher than the mind; and he [the soul] is even higher than the intelligence."

~*~

Love is not rational and it goes beyond intelligence.

It is in our nature, in your nature.

The greatest deviation from our loving being to our perception-like lifestyle choices comes from our unwillingness to be present, to connect with the transcendental source of this unity in which this Universe flows.

~*~

If we could, just for a moment, release the resistance caused by beliefs and assumptions, we would discover the powerful flame of love in our hearts, in our spirits, like a flame that can only expand providing, helping, inspiring, assisting, embracing, touching, caring for, connecting, blending, and unifying us with others.

Only love breaks the illusion of separation. Doing small things, such as smiling to every person you cross paths with, assisting in some type of service, caring for someone in need, truly listening, in other words, bringing an awareness of your capability to create bonds with others in the present moment. You experience the ecstasy when there is no fear or resistance to what you truly are in essence: powerful loving beings.

Applying the power of love cannot ever be counterproductive. Love awakens our physical power to heal. Love brings the true meaning of unity to our awareness, in which we are all sharing the same world, in the same Universe, far beyond into the infinite source of creation that God *is*.

Love *is* our direct communion with God.

Imagine your spirit as a single flame. This flame grows brighter every time love is activated in the energy centers of your body, your chakras. You feel that warmth embracing you, separating you from the limitations of time and space. You are giving love. You want to continue with this feeling and you realize that by doing this you can transfer light from your single flame to other people's flames. Their hearts are enlightened by your precious love.

~*~

Your flame grows when you experience that a chain of communion starts to grow from your single flame. Those who feel inspired by you continue their journey, sharing their flames with others.

~*~

An act of love expands; it never dies. It is through this feeling of inner-connection with the divine source that a love chain reaction can be started. Those who you share your flame with can combine their flames with others, growing in intensity and sharing love with those who are drawn to the same experience. By serving others love can only grow—never diminish.

Yet somehow you believe there are limits to this precious energy of your soul. If you believe that being loving and helpful to others can make you feel weak and exhausted, then your flame is weak due to your unwillingness to transform your illusions. In that case, focus on bringing the true power of intention to envision new opportunities for you to activate your soul and share its light. You are capable of being loving at any moment, because that is who you really are when the illusions of time and space are released and you surrender to the flow of pure Love.

Can you remember moments in which true love was being experienced and time seemed to stop? Moments when your body seemed to blend with someone else's body? Of course you do because you have trained your mind to believe that it is only through sex that you can achieve such a profound state of love. Is that really your truth? Are there other ways you can love that are not related to physical pleasure?

Love is a healing force, a miracle for the ego mind that once co-created a world where love was limited to kisses and sexual intimacy. True love is that and much more. Dare to experience love by giving it through small acts. Be kind. Be honest. Be peaceful. Be of assistance in any opportunity you are being introduced to by this amazing flow of the Universe, because that is when awareness blesses your heart. Time is an illusion. So is any limitation.

~*~

Your reality is shaped by the way you intend to live your present moment. Intend to love by surrendering to the wisdom of your spirit, which only wants happiness for you and everyone you share your existence with.

~*~

Every so-called problem in our lives is just another opportunity to sow, in you and in others, the seeds of kindness, honesty, compassion, truthfulness, integrity, co-creative power, and enthusiasm.

It is a matter of choice. You are always free to change the way you think and, consequently, what you think will allow another feeling to take place. If you are having a "bad" day you can start by understanding that absolutely everything that is happening to you in your day is a reflection of your co-creative power, of your ability to attract opportunities into your life. By acknowledging a "bad" day you are projecting negative thoughts and feelings in the present moment. You can always choose the way your thoughts are being directed. Change the way you think and the way you feel will change as well. Now, there is no such a thing as "problems," only situations—opportunities for you to express your wonderful wisdom.

~*~

Think of light as the manifestation of your molecules dancing in love; think of love as food for your spirit.

There is so much beauty to be enjoyed.

Make contact with your soul's appetite and cook for it.

Use passion as the flame that heats up your life.

~*~

Rediscover your ability to desire from your heart's purpose. Make love with your dreams and bring them alive with every single step you walk upon this earth.

Only by raising your level of consciousness to a higher frequency can you actually feel better. Follow your guidance to feel better, always doing the things you truly love. You are only able to truly see what you are in harmony with. If you think about depression the unwanted frequencies of the emotions attached to that state will be reflected all around you. If you focus on gratitude grace will take over; these feelings of gratitude will raise your vibrational field and you will find yourself in a state of appreciation, which the dense frequencies of depression cannot disrupt.

Think about this: absolutely every single event in your life and all the people you have ever met were there only because you drew them into your field of experiences. It is your exclusive task to do with them what you please, just do not forget that there is a deeper meaning, which may be discovered instantaneously or even decades later. All the circumstances of your life bring you wisdom and blessings; it is in the way of perceiving them that you may find reasons to feel uncertainty. It is in your potential to love that you can find the meaning of your life.

~*~ *The answer to all your callings is love.* ~*~

Spiritual Workout 9

Practice random acts of love.

You can aim big but start with small acts of love that speak for themselves. You can begin by being loving to those closest to you.

Today, greet everyone with a smile.

Be randomly kind: to an employee that seems unhappy with their job, make them smile; tell them something nice to remind them about their beauty; give a gift to someone today; buy healthy food for someone that needs it, instead of telling them they should eat healthier; choose to focus on what you like about your family and friends rather than what you despise, and encourage them to keep it up. Give your food leftovers to the pigeons or squirrels instead of throwing it away, as you think about being one of them. How happy would you feel if someone gave you fresh food when you were hungry? Do not wait for a special occasion to call the people you love. Share smiles and become a helpful participant in someone else's adventure.

In meditation, open your heart, and visualize the flame of your spirit. There are many meditation techniques that will help you connect with the Universe. One of my favorite ones is focusing only on feelings of appreciation and unity—feeling connected with everything that surrounds me always through gratitude. Breathe light. In other words, connect with the beauty of nature as it connects to your breath. You are essentially connected to the flowers, plants, pets, other people, the sky, the clouds, the stars, etc., you just have to close your eyes and feel the illusion of separateness fall away.

Practice this as much as possible during your day, without forcing yourself to do it. If you are going to meditate, free yourself from your routine, and make sure there will be no interferences such as phone calls. You will feel better if you allow yourself to enjoy a few minutes of meditation everyday without any kind of resistance from your thoughts.

Conclusion

This concludes the ninth power to transform your life. In this journey to awaken these powers within, you will find the magnificent opportunities that this wave of synchronicity has to offer. The more you practice these Nine Powers the more you will discover their miraculous repercussions, and the more you will meet with the circumstances that your heart desires. Trust in the wisdom of your spirit. Your intuitions are based on sacred guidance that is always answering your calling.

You are capable of being as happy as you have always wanted to be. You can start where you are right now, because now is the perfect moment to do so. Transcend all types of excuses, for they come from your fears. You can change your habits if they are not contributing to your wellbeing.

I would like to summarize the *Nine Powers* into one wave in which each Power blends with the others. There is no special sequence in which you must practice them, though it may seem that there is a natural flow from one to the other. In your journey, you will discover which Powers you are already practicing and which ones you need to put more attention on.

I guarantee that the Nine Powers will transform your life, and bring you peace, joy, faith, hope, and wealth. You will discover the sacred source from which you came, the one and only, to which all of us are connected. You will enjoy each opportunity that arises, each moment in your life, as a reflection of your inner relationship with this divine source, and you will express your magnificent contributions to the wellbeing of humanity.

The Nine Powers to Transform Your Life are:

 The Power of Decision

 The Power of Forgiveness

 The Power of Intention

 The Power of Purpose

 The Power of Appreciation

 The Power of Will

 The Power of Passion

 The Power of Beauty

 The Power of Love

Every experience in your path is coming in response to your choices. Choose wisely, respecting who you really are.

Conclusion

Awake your Power of Decision.

Chose wisely by instantaneously feeling better inviting the new opportunity to shift your consciousness to the state of clarity, of knowing what your heart truly desires and to trusting it by stepping forward in its direction. Remember that fears come from a belief of lack, another type of thought that makes you weak. Change the small things that contribute as fuel for each old habit, transmuting them into the new habits that are in harmony with what your being really wants.

Most health problems come from resentment and resistance to change. The great news is that you have the Power of Forgiveness and this power is greater than any situation that may have hurt you. The sooner you forgive, the sooner you will become healthier and happier in every way. Let sacred guidance lead you to a place where you can heal the wounds in your heart. You are always in the right place whether you want it or not; there are revelations for you to discover wherever you may be. The ability to act from love and forgiveness will bless your experience, and will definitely begin healing your life.

Blame only invites resistance into your life's experiences and expands more pain all over your emotional and physical body. Once you act with the power of forgiveness, a sense of joy and peace blesses your body allowing its exceptional response to heal every emotional wound. You can always choose peace instead of resentment. It is your choice.

Set yourself free from past experiences charges of negative emotions. By living here and now, you release the emotional pain retained from past experiences, and you manifest the transmutation from fear to love, from pain to healing. You can transform your mind if you only release your resistance to love by forgiving yourself and others.

Raise your emotional state to feel better, without blaming, just forgiving and manifesting, from now on, only the experiences you want to live. You can only live now, so why bother to pretend you are living in the past? Take responsibility for the way you feel, since no one else is responsible for "making" you feel that way—only you are, by the way you choose to think. The great news is that there is absolutely nothing you cannot transform in your mind. Surrender to love. Any resistance can only bring illusion and fear. It is the ego mind perception state that is responsible for any pain in your body, and it wants to always be right. Your spirit only wants to be kind, to be compassionate, and to be forgiving.

What we think, we are. It is in the way we think that we become. Express your clarity by living in alignment with your aspirations. Use your Power of Intention by choosing to have the thoughts that are in harmony with the kind of inspired life you want to live. Intend what it is that you would really like to attract whether it is wonderful relationships or great communication with family and friends and everyone that you share your moments with, and start by working on it, from inside out. Your intention shapes your focus, guiding you always to know how well balanced you are in relation with your heart's desire.

True happiness blesses every cell in your body when you are inspired by a powerful intention of living with a sense of mission, of purpose, of accomplishing something extraordinary in cooperation with others. Your talents are the tools to build your heart's desire, to assist your soul's purpose in the blending with other people's purposes.

When you manifest your God-given gifts there is no place for unhappiness. There is no such thing as loneliness when you perform with your Power of Purpose. There is a universal song that you are a part of and you are also the composer of one of its verses—your mission. Your verse is not small. It is as big and important as the rest of the verses. Remember always to match your purpose with your talents since they work better together.

Choose to invest your energy in expressing your talents more often. Share them with the world. Your wonderful gifts can help others raise their wellbeing vibrations. Your talents are melodies that combined with other people's talents create a symphony. Work to find a tune between your talents and the talents of those around you.

Harmony comes from your expression of your purpose in communion with the rest of the orchestra, when you add your tunes to the universal song. If your talents are aligned with your purpose, the Universe opens up for you. You will attract into your life the magnificent opportunities to play your music. In the process of consciousness expansion we are all one. Act upon your purpose. You already know there is a purpose for you to be here and now.

The closer you focus from your purpose, the better you feel, instantly and the easier it will be to awake the *Power of Appreciation*. Expressing your connection with other people's purposes through appreciation contributes to increasing their enthusiasm to feel better. If you can focus upon what you like in something, rather than what you dislike, your power of appreciation will do the rest and bless your moment with joy.

Feelings of gratitude raise your overall wellbeing vibration. Every time you gratefully connect with your senses, your mind, your body, and spirit and you smile, appreciating their importance, your immune system produces the necessary energy to keep you strong, healthy, and dynamic. By starting each day saying, "Thank you God! This is a great day! Thank you for this opportunity to love again!" You know it will be a beautiful day, because you chose it to be that way.

It is only by expressing your gratitude to every single contribution necessary for your expansion that you are in tune with the big movie you are directing. Your happiness arises from that level of appreciation. Feel the warmth and love from all that surrounds you and blends with you.

Conclusion

When you appreciate something your spiritual energy expands with the appreciated thing. Use your powerful appreciation of the fact that you can breathe, look at the sky, let the sunshine caress your face, feel the blessing of having another day to dream, plan, and move on your way with gratitude.

Appreciation transcends the judgemental mind state just by being thankful for the knowledge every circumstance provides, even if you do not find a meaningful message at that moment. By focusing only on what you appreciate from others you will find the way of attracting the necessary peace to avoid the battles of ego and manipulation.

Appreciation not only makes you aware of other people's contributions, but also inspires your sincere compliments to raise other's wellbeing energy. Only fear can alter your appreciation state letting doubts get stronger, and alter your perception of the environment dimensions.

The more fears and doubts you have, the more opportunities you will have to overcome them, to awaken the Power of Will. Remember your spirit needs to enrich from the environment's energy to keep calm and emotional balance. If you work to discover your own denial mechanisms you will find the way to face your fears, to live in peace with everything that surrounds you. As long as you know what you really want, you will know what you heart needs. You will be able to eliminate the idea of failure and doubts because you will trust that everything occurs according to the opportunities you keep attracting—to awaken the power of your will. Each fear is productive because it gives you the opportunity of activating your self-confidence and developing your will.

Each fear is there to teach you something. You have the power to do whatever you really aim to do. You have the will to dispel any fear that appears. The only thing that stops you is your own resistance to change. The overcoming of your fears is only possible by taking responsibility, as it is you who give them power over your actions. Whatever it is you want to do, do it today. When the opportunity arrives, answer the call. Allow the experience to enter your field of attraction fully. Trust your will's ability to reach your goals. Remember always that what you think, as well as what you fear, manifests.

The only way for us to understand the message hidden in our fears is in facing them. Have a conversation with them. Look at the imaginary world you are creating behind them with each of your perceptions. See everything as if you were out of your body and then use the power of your will to get ready to conquer your feeling of inability. Do whatever works for you, but face them and transcend each of them one by one. Be aware of your own mental barriers and imagined limits. Once you notice your own reluctance to accomplish your goals, you will have the opportunity to make a different choice. Act with enthusiasm and change the way you do things using the power of your will.

Conclusion

Use the Power of Passion to seize the day without any procrastination.

You cannot attract love by doing things you do not love. Decide what you want to attract into your life and start living passionately. Start doing it with all your heart and body. Enthusiasm is the key to manifesting your heart's desires. If you focus on living passionately you will learn to enjoy everything that surrounds you. Envision the life you really want to live using the previous powers and visualize it happening in the now. Use your senses to manifest the passionate feeling of living your heart's desire as it is really happening now. Keep this vision and smile as if you have already achieved it.

The Power of Passion raises your creativity and helps you expand your talent by attracting serendipity into your life adventure. Nothing can divert you from your inner path unless you allow it. You are responsible for any deflection. Remember meaningless accidents do not exist. Every accident leads us to a recognition related to change. You are the director of your movie, your adventure, and only you can choose whom to share it with. Spread your passion for what you do to others, share your smile, and remain focused on the experiences that lead you to create something new.

The magical passion of using your talents will lead you to inspire others, and, when you least expect it, the people you interact with will be vibrating in similar frequencies of spiritual cooperation with you. You will be able to see that many people feel happy about having attracted the successful experience of sharing their talents with you. You will realize that teamwork generates higher levels of consciousness.

If you change the way you have always thought about your body, your physical image will change in your own eyes. It is that simple. However, it requires a type of attention that invites in the feeling of "I am beautiful" as the secret ingredient. Be aware of the loving and beautiful being that you are and share it with passion. Reveal your true beauty by awakening the Power of Beauty.

To be detached from people's opinions is a wonderful and necessary daily practice on your path towards your inner and beautiful self. Self-confidence is a major step in developing a healthy lifestyle. You do not need anyone to tell you how beautiful you are because you already know it. If you keep asking others for approval you are depending on their opinions for your happiness. If you start loving yourself your beauty will radiate out its true power.

Nearly everyday we have the chance to transform, just like an alchemist, any material into gold, any feeling or situation into beauty. If you act from beauty, you will see beauty reflecting back at you. There is a land of beauty to be discovered in all of us. Intend everyday to explore the beauty of those around you and inspire them with passion to express it.

There is love in you and being in touch with it will transform your vibrational field. You will start to feel safe and this feeling of safety will transform your energy to help you grow to be more hopeful and receptive. There is so much beauty around and inside you that if you observe and connect to it you will receive the necessary energy to be able to take a deep breath and return to love, your natural state of wellbeing.

Feeling the beauty, appreciating its true power, reminds us of the importance of loving ourselves as the necessary step before we can love others. It is through small acts of love that we can awaken the *Power of Love*. Begin by being loving to those closest to you. Greet everyone with a smile and enjoy being randomly kind: to an employee that seems unhappy with their current circumstances, make them smile, tell them something nice to remind them of their beauty; give a gift to someone more often; choose to focus on awakening the beauty and loving core in your family and friends rather than what you do not like in them, and encourage them to be for-giving. Give your food leftovers to the pigeons or squirrels instead of throwing it away, as you think about you being one of them, understanding the transcendental power of love in which even a pigeon needs to be treated with love. Relate to every life form imagining how it is to live in their bodies and appreciate their existence.

We are all helpful participants in someone else's adventure. Blend your love with everyone you cross paths with. Love can only be experienced by the act of loving. Our essence is shaped in eternity and blends in unity. Separation only comes from ideas, limitations, unawareness, fear—from all that lacks the expression of the Power of Love. Love goes beyond intelligence; you do not need to be a scholar to act with this most profound power. Love awakens our physical power to heal. Love brings the true meaning of unity to our awareness, in which we are all shifting our consciousness, realizing the divine source of creation that God *is*. Love *is* our direct communion with the divine source in each of us, with God.

By serving others, love can only expand and grow, never diminish. Your reality is shaped by the way you intend to live your present moment. Intend to love by surrendering to the wisdom of your spirit that only wants happiness for you and everyone you share your existence with.

Every so-called "problem" in our lives is just another opportunity to express your love through kindness, honesty, compassion, truthfulness, integrity, co-creative power, and enthusiasm.

It is always a matter of choice. By changing the way you think you will allow another feeling to take place. Everything that is happening to you in your day is a reflection of your co-creative power, of your ability to attract opportunities into your life. There are no such a thing as "problems," only situations, results, and opportunities for you to express your wonderful wisdom. Rediscover your ability to desire from your heart's purpose. Make love with your dreams and bring them alive with every single step you walk upon this earth.

Conclusion

You can always raise your level of consciousness to a higher frequency to feel better if you follow your guidance, doing the things you truly love. You are only able to truly see what you are in harmony with. If you think about something that lowers your wellbeing energy the unwanted frequencies of the emotions attached to that state will be reflected all around you. If you focus on something that inspires gratitude grace will bless you. These feelings of gratitude will raise you vibrational field and you will find yourself in a state of appreciation, where the Power of Love can arise stronger.

All the happenings of your life bring you wisdom and blessings. It is in your way of perceiving them that you may find reasons to feel uncertainty. It is in your potential to love that you can find the meaning of each situation in your journey to self-fulfilment. Love is in your nature, as in the nature of everything that was created. If you let it be, just for a moment, by releasing the resistance caused by ego-based perceptions of reality, you will discover the powerful Power of Love in everyone's hearts, in their sacred spirits—like a flame that can only expand providing, helping, inspiring, assisting, embracing, touching, caring for, connecting, blending, and unifying all of us.

If you do this, you will discover the sacred source from which you and I and everything comes, the one and only force that connects us all. You will enjoy each opportunity that springs forth by practicing these Nine Powers as a reflection of your inner relationship with the divine source, and you will express your magnificent contributions to the wellbeing of humanity. The more you use your powers along the way, you will eliminate all barriers and limitations from your own perceptions, freeing you from resistance and allowing your shift in consciousness.

There is so much beauty in you. Follow your powers. Enjoy this journey, and, most importantly, feel wonderful about it.

~*~

Thank you, Guidance. Thank you, Universe. Thank you, God...and thank You.

With Love and Blessings,
~*~ Nicolás Nóbile ~*~

About the Author

Nicolás Nóbile is a skilled and experienced lecturer, teacher, and spiritual teacher. He has appeared on the radio and television in the Chicagoland areas as a Feng Shui and holistic medicine advisor. Born and reared in Argentina, Nicolás began as a visual artist, which led him to Eastern art and finally Eastern healing medicine. He has worked nationally and internationally as a Reiki Master, Pakua instructor, Oriental medicine practitioner and inspirational lecturer. He is not aligned with any particular religion and his message is based in transcedental experiences which have led him to seek to inspire millions of people around the globe. For more information about Nicolás and his work go to www.alquimia9.com.

LaVergne, TN USA
23 February 2011
217702LV00001B/1/P